THE GRAD SCHOOL HANDBOOK

THE GRAD SCHOOL HANDBOOK

An INSIDER'S GUIDE to GETTING IN and SUCCEEDING

RICHARD JERRARD and
MARGOT JERRARD

A PERIGEE BOOK

A Perigee Book
Published by The Berkley Publishing Group
A member of Penguin Putnam Inc.
200 Madison Avenue
New York, NY 10016

First edition: July 1998

Published simultaneously in Canada.

The Penguin Putnam Inc. World Wide Web site address is
http://www.penguinputnam.com

Library of Congress Cataloging-in-Publication Data

Jerrard, Richard.
The grad school handbook / Richard Jerrard and Margot Jerrard.—
1st ed.
p. cm.
"A Perigee book."
ISBN 0-399-52416-9
1. Universities and colleges—United States—Graduate work—
Handbooks, manuals, etc. 2. Universities and colleges—United
States—Graduate work—Admission—Handbooks, manuals, etc.
3. Graduate students—United States—Handbooks, manuals, etc.
I. Jerrard, Margot. II. Title.
LB2371.4.J47 1998
371.55'0973—dc21   97-40764
                                                      CIP

Printed in the United States of America

10 9 8 7 6 5 4 3 2 1

CONTENTS

PREFACE

THIS BOOK WILL take you to graduate school. From choosing the right school to paying for your degree, we'll show you how to get in and how to succeed once you're there. In our years of work in graduate education, we have seen the inside story of admissions, assistantship and fellowship awards, appointment of teaching assistants, graduate examinations, and the rest. We'll give you the inside scoop on how to make sure you're at the front of the line for admission and financial aid.

A few notes on terminology: Universities differ widely in their administrative titles though the jobs are similar. We will refer to the boss of a program as the Head, the day-to-day administrative officer as the Associate Head. The administrator most concerned with graduate students, who keeps track of the academic progress of graduate students and may also be the chief recruiting officer, is usually called the Director of Graduate Studies or the Graduate Adviser.

This book is going to help you to know how the system works. We want to give you information that will be vital in applying for admission and financial aid, and in singling yourself out as a top graduate student.

Good luck in your graduate career.

ACKNOWLEDGMENTS

WE WERE HELPED in this work by many faculty members and former and current graduate students around the country. Among them were Eric Breitbart, University of Notre Dame; Kate Denevan, University of Minnesota; John Drabble, University of California at Berkeley; Carol Green, Boston College; Laura Jerrard, University of California at Berkeley; Leigh Jerrard, University of Illinois; Robert Jerrard, University of California at Berkeley; Andreas Kreifel, Union College; Susan May, Brown University; Kitty Millett, California State University at Long Beach; L. Jackson Newell, University of Utah; Pat O'Connor, University of Chicago; Bertrand Poritsky, Columbia University; and Joseph Szewczak, Deep Springs College.

We also had the benefit of help from many colleagues at the University of Illinois. These included Cheryl Berger, J. Gary Eden, Frank Gladney, Caroline Hibbard, Jane Loeb, Judy McCulloh, Carol Neely, Bruce Reznick, Leon Waldoff, and Gaye Wong.

Finally, we are grateful to our editors, Stefanie Antoine and Jeremy Katz, for their very useful suggestions.

PART 1 FIRST THINGS

CHAPTER 1

WHY GRADUATE SCHOOL?

> *It was the best thing I ever did. I needed a job, and for that I needed credentials. Getting the M.B.A. was exciting. It was challenging to put together all the new things that I learned in a very different area from my undergraduate degree. And when I finished I got this great job as business manager for a surgical supply company, and I knew how to handle it.*
>
> —*JEANIE*

AN EXCITING FUTURE and a job you love can be yours. If you want to do work that you enjoy and earn more money, graduate or professional school can be the way.

A graduate degree gives you a big advantage. When you complete a master's, doctoral, or professional degree you are a skilled individual, someone who is valuable in today's job market, a person with ability who has taken the time and effort to earn the degree.

Graduate school shows you how to make the most of yourself. It will help you to forge a stimulating life, whether you are an undergraduate who wants to move ahead of the pack, or are in mid-career and want to change your life around. Not only will you be better educated, but you will become an expert in your field. A highly skilled person gets respect on the job and from society, as well as more money and career mobility. Employers are looking for highly trained people who can communicate what they have learned.

If you have been out of college for a few years, working in jobs with no future, a graduate degree will have the effect of wiping out the past. When you have a new master's degree, people do not care how you spent your earlier years.

Many studies have shown that the successful, highly paid people in today's economy are the "symbol manipulators." This is what you are if you are a writer, a lawyer, a professor, a computer programmer, or are in any profession requiring creative mental work. A graduate degree will give you specific skills as well as the confidence that comes with them.

Not all of the following advice will apply to everyone. Your particular situation will depend on the program you undertake and on the school you attend. Certain professional programs have clear-cut steps you must take one at a time, while many doctoral programs emphasize original research. Read on; take and use the information that is helpful to you.

HELP IS ON THE WAY

This book will show you how to get into the best program for you.

Getting into graduate school is different from applying to a college. Graduate work focuses on a single field. Instead of going through a standardized process that is the same for all applicants, as you did before attending college, and being admitted by a committee of the whole university, you apply directly to the program in which you will be studying, and you are selected or refused by people in that department. You have to convince the individual professors that they want you and that you deserve financial aid.

This book takes you through the process step by step, and shows you how to get in and succeed. We have worked with graduate students, and in the Graduate College of the University of Illinois at Urbana-Champaign for years. We have made the crucial admission decisions, and have helped many students through all stages from beginning the search to receiving the degree. We have the insider's point of view and can tell you what really happens and how decisions are made inside the universities.

One of us, Richard Jerrard, has been Director of Graduate Studies at the University of Illinois department of mathematics in Urbana, which has over 200 graduate students. Richard has read thousands of applications and played a key role in his department and in the university's Graduate College in deciding which applicants to admit and which ones will get financial aid. Margot Jerrard has written handbooks, newsletters, and catalogs for graduate students. We have both talked to students past and present at many universities, to faculty members and to administrators and deans, and from their experiences have learned things you will not learn from any other source.

This book tells you:

- how to get information you need,
- what to look for in the programs you are considering,
- how to evaluate programs and select the right one for you,
- the best sources of financial aid, and how to get it,
- how to write a winning essay,
- how to get good references,
- ways to prepare for the GRE or the other professional tests you will have to take,
- who makes the admission decisions and what they are looking for, and
- how to succeed once you are in.

The following chapters will show you procedures to follow that will help you to get admitted, and how to get off to a good start once you are in graduate school. Some information, particularly about areas of research and financial aid, will not apply to students in certain professional programs. Just take and use whatever applies to your situation. The last chapters tell you how to get the most out of graduate school, how to solve problems that arise, and how to make your graduate education a big success.

LEARNING HOW TO THINK

When you are in graduate school you have smaller classes and seminars, with many occasions to talk to your professors. You work and study with other graduate students. Even at a big university, you are a member of a small community of people working in the same area. There is an excitement that the faculty feel about their subject, an excitement they want to impart to the students.

Graduate school is challenging and will mean working hard, devoting days and often nights to work. The standards demanded of you will be higher than they were when you were in college. It will mean not joining nonstudent friends when they go off for a weekend in the mountains and, instead, staying home to work in the library. Late hours spent poring over texts, nights working in a lab or studio or at the computer until the sun rises, will not be uncommon. When you were an undergraduate the emphasis was on examinations and grades. Now, you will need to understand your whole field. It's hard work, but rewarding and exciting.

Susan May, whose Ph.D. from Brown University is in physiology and biophysics, found being in graduate school stimulating. "Being a graduate student is a wonderful life. You are with fascinating people. You get immersed in a program and learn how to think."

For Susan, as for many others, being a graduate student was a happy experience. Graduate students do not have enough money, work hard, labor against stiff competition, and feel uneasy about future job prospects. However, they are learning something they are interested in and associating with people who have the same interests. Even though they feel uncertainty about the future, most students enjoy these years in school. They are progressing toward a goal. They like the comradeship with other students and being with faculty who are excited about their discoveries.

MASTER'S OR DOCTORATE?

They are quite different. Which is the one for you?

Most graduate students work toward a master's degree. The best known degrees are Master of Arts (M.A.) and Master of Science (M.S.), but there is a huge variety of others. Some are designed to lead to an eventual doctoral degree. Many other master's candidates are in professional programs, preparing for a special kind of work, such as the Master of Business Administration, Master of Social Work, or the Master of Architecture.

Doctoral degrees are the highest degrees attainable and come in two types; a doctor of philosophy (Ph.D.) is training for research and is required if you want to become a professor in a university, although probably more than half the people who hold Ph.D.s are not employed by universities. Almost every high-level scientific researcher has a Ph.D. degree. Other doctoral degrees fit you to work in a certain profession, such as Doctor of Education (D.Ed.) or Doctor of Musical Arts (D.M.A.). Some of these are not research degrees, but generally you must write a substantial thesis. The M.D. and the J.D. (Juris Doctor, the usual law school degree) do not require a thesis. For these professional fields, each school's requirements are quite specific.

MASTER'S DEGREE

A master's degree is required for many positions in education, social work, and public health. It will definitely help you to get a job in mathematics, computer science, engineering, architecture, or business. It will help you to get a promotion or a higher salary if you are a teacher. Most people who get master's degrees are in education, business, or engineering; they want a good position, to be upgraded in their present jobs, or to change professions. On the other hand, an M.A. in philosophy or English will make you more employable, but will not train you for work in any specific field. However, all other things being equal, an employer who wants to fill a position that requires writing skills will prefer an applicant with a master's degree to one with a bachelor's.

People with master's degrees in history or English find good jobs in public relations, broadcasting, researching for documentaries, information offices, government intelligence and foreign service, among other fields. Others who want to travel get a master's in the teaching of English as a Second Language, which leads to jobs teaching English in many foreign countries.

Generally it will take a full-time student from one and a half to three years, depending on the program, to complete the work for a master's degree. The requirements are usually clearly spelled out; you have definite courses in certain areas and examinations to pass at certain times. The degree may also require a master's thesis. Sometimes this involves original research on your part. Other times a thesis for a master's degree means that you must write a substantial expository paper on some topic that is suggested to you. In that case you don't have to break new ground or generate ideas that are worthy of publication. Working on a master's degree does not require the years or the money needed to get a doctorate.

One benefit of a master's degree is that it can enable you to change directions completely. You can make a new start and begin a different career. If you find that you are no longer interested in the psychology you majored in during college, you can apply to a completely new field, such as architecture, and with an M.Arch. start work as an architect. Or, if your English major is not leading you to the kinds of jobs you want, you can change goals and work on a master's in public health.

Many departments have different tracks, one for those whose graduate work continues on straight from their undergraduate studies and another for people making a career switch. If you are contemplating a big change, that track will enable you to make up the courses you didn't have. It may take you longer to get the degree than it will take those who majored in that subject, but for a lot of people a master's degree can be a new start in life.

DOCTORAL DEGREE

In some professions a Ph.D. or some other doctoral degree is your entry card. It is a requirement for almost every college professor. But keep in mind that about half the people who have doctoral degrees find interesting, well-paying work away from college teaching. If your goal is to do scholarly or high-level scientific research in a field such as chemistry, engineering, or economics, a Ph.D. is required. Ph.D.s in mathematics work for investment firms on Wall Street (and earn much higher salaries than their former classmates who are assistant professors). Ph.D.s in economics work for big corporations, or for state or federal government agencies. Others who hold doctorates are the directors of big libraries or art museums, or geologists who travel to exotic places to find minerals or to study the physical history of our planet.

In a Ph.D. program you are trained to be a scholar or researcher in the field and are awarded your doctorate after you pass the examinations and complete a thesis that shows original research. This means years of study, and writing a dissertation that is then read and criticized by a committee of scholars.

For this degree you will need to work independently and to take the initiative for your research. Some students who have done brilliantly in their undergraduate and graduate class work flounder when it comes to the independent research required for a doctoral dissertation. Others thrive on this challenge and enjoy working ahead on their own.

The requirements for a doctorate are not as specific as for a master's. You have a much wider choice of course work, and the choice of research area can be daunting. Sometimes it is difficult to find out in detail what the requirements for the doctorate are. You not only have to complete certain courses, but also pass examinations whose subject and form may not be completely specified, and then, most crucial, find a mentor, an adviser who will help you to write a good dissertation. Plans of attack for these situations are covered in later chapters.

MAXIMIZING YOUR CHANCES

In some departments all students must begin as master's candidates even if they plan to continue on until they receive the doctorate. If you go into one of those programs, you have to complete the course work and examinations for the master's degree before you will be officially admitted to the Ph.D. program. However, the department will know if you are ultimately working toward a Ph.D., if that is your goal. In other programs you can go straight to a Ph.D. without even getting a master's degree.

In most academic departments in which both a Ph.D. and a master's are awarded, you have a choice. You can apply either to be admitted as a master's candidate or as a potential Ph.D. Which should you choose?

You will have more chance of getting financial aid if you start as a doctoral candidate rather than a master's candidate. There are exceptions, but usually academic departments award little financial aid to master's candidates. Most support goes to students who are in the Ph.D. program, which takes much longer to complete.

If you are not certain whether you will stop with a master's or continue toward a doctorate, make it clear on your application that your goal is a doctorate even if you are not sure how far you want to go. However, if you feel that you are unlikely to be admitted as a doctoral candidate, applying as a master's candidate can increase your chances of admission.

Many departments have different standards for doctoral and master's students. They will accept some applicants in a master's program they do not consider good enough to admit to the Ph.D. program. If you have been rejected for a Ph.D. program by the department you really want, you can telephone the Graduate Adviser and ask to be admitted to work on a master's. Then, if you do an outstanding job as a master's student, you may be able to persuade the faculty to change their minds and let you stay on to work for the doctorate.

IS A DOCTORATE WORTH IT?

If you want to be a college teacher, is it worth the effort to get a Ph.D. now when universities are cutting back on their hiring and are even closing academic departments? Definitely, if you are interested in the subject and—this is important—are willing to be flexible about your ultimate position. There is a strong demand for good, knowledgeable people with expertise and needed skills, even in this time of downsizing.

Many people find that with their doctoral degrees they get good jobs, even though they are not teaching at a university.

Matt has a Ph.D. in mathematics from Virginia, which garnered him an assistant professorship at a remote college. Dissatisfied, he went to Wall Street, where he is now an authority on predicting which technical stocks to invest in. Van, whose Ph.D. was in English, has a high-level job in public relations for a big company. Mary, with a Ph.D. in mineral economics, has worked for both the government and big business in between the births of her three children. Annette, with a doctorate in education, works for a combined hospital and clinic. She conducts workshops and classes that teach employees the best ways to interact with patients and with other staff members.

TAKING STOCK

How do you know which programs to apply for? Start by evaluating your situation:

- What work do you hope to do?
- What are your chances of success?
- What are your abilities and interests?

Also be sure to answer the evaluation questions at the end of the chapter. The next chapter tells you how to get the information you will need to make a choice.

Most people who consider graduate school, including many of the most successful ones, have a strong interest in their subject before they start graduate work, and also have confidence in their ability to do work at that level.

THE WORK YOU ARE AIMING FOR

Your first decision is to determine your goal. Decide what work you want to do and how you'd like to spend your life.

For some students there is no question.

Marina always knew she would go to graduate school and what she would study. She loved animals. When as a child she found out that she could actually get paid for working with them, she had no doubt that was for her. Marina went straight from college, having earned good grades in the courses she needed, to graduate school at the University of Texas at Austin. She is now a young assistant professor who spends every summer in Africa, observing monkeys, doing the work she has always wanted to do.

Other people are not nearly so certain.

While working on her B.A. in college, Janet had not been much interested in classwork, and her grades were not very good. All she had wanted to do was get married. At the age of thirty-two, in a shaky marriage with two small children, she knew that now she had to finish her education. She needed to prepare herself for a job that would earn a living, and she wanted one that she liked doing.

After being out of school for years, she found it difficult to return. There were examinations to study for, papers to write, projects to complete. At times she didn't know if she could continue. She did. Now she is a dean at a Big Ten university, who works with graduate students.

As Janet found out, going back to school to work on a graduate degree can be exhausting. However, if this is the field you want to devote your life to, some dedication and hard work now will pay off with a satisfying job in the future.

But then there are the people who have no clear idea of what to do after their bachelor's degree. Burt was one.

Burt had to do something, but he didn't know what. He only knew that after three and a half years at his Big Ten university he did not like to read or write, and especially did not like to give reports. He thought he'd stay on, continue living at the fraternity and go to law school. Since his freshman year it had been easy for him to get fairly good grades without doing much work. He was smart but also lazy.

But law schools are very selective. Students cannot coast through. They spend long hours each week reading about cases and torts and contracts. When Burt talked to law students, he began to wonder if this was for him. When he found out how much work it would be just to prepare his applications, he realized that he was not ready. He took a year off to travel through Europe and to think about what he really wanted to do.

Deciding to go to graduate school because you do not know what else to do, and spending years and thousands of dollars, is not a good idea. It is too much work and too hard to keep going if you are not really interested. If you don't have a clear idea, wait until you do.

YOUR PATH TO SUCCESS

The next step is to learn as much as possible about your chances of succeeding in that field once you have the degree.

Some people know that they want to earn more money. Others want to enter a profession where high achievement will earn autonomy, independence, or a feeling of accomplishment. They may want to teach or work in scientific research or for an art museum. While you cannot see the future, you can apply some general principles. If you decide to be an artist, chances are you will have more trouble making a lot of money than if you are a banker. But if art is your passion, you can give it a good try.

Elizabeth, a graduate student in astronomy, had always loved music and supported herself partly by playing the organ every Sunday at a local church. While she liked astronomy, she loved music. After a while she realized that the only thing she really wanted to study was music. She saw that her friends in astronomy were not having an easy time getting jobs and decided to work on a Ph.D. in music theory. She's a graduate music student now, and doesn't know what her life will be like financially, but she is doing what she wants to do.

Some people do make a living as artists. After you think it over, you may decide to take the risk and apply to Master of Fine Arts programs in painting. You might become a recognized painter, or an illustrator. Or perhaps you will choose a field in which you can use your artistic ability at a job, such as industrial design, or computer graphics.

Lori decided to study for a master's in art. While in school she took several courses in computer graphics. As soon as she received her master's she went to California, where she is now a highly paid computer graphic artist.

Ray, who had drawn pictures from the time he could hold a crayon in preschool, received a master's in medical illustrating. He found a job in a university department of anatomy and, as he worked there, became interested in the subject. He wanted to learn more and returned to school to get a Ph.D. in anatomy. He now is a professor who teaches anatomy to medical students, in addition to medical illustrating. He has produced four illustrated anatomy books, which combine his interests and supplement his income.

CAN YOU DO IT?

Graduate school is an enormous commitment of time, money, energy and effort. It is important to make an informed choice.

Take a piece of paper, think about these questions, and write down your answers.

- What are my career goals?
- Master's or doctorate?
- Am I interested enough in the subject to stay with it for two or three or six years?
- Do I have the energy and commitment to work hard for as long as it takes?
- Can I take the pressure?
- Can I find the money to pay tuition, living expenses, and books?
- Can I make satisfactory arrangements for my family?
- Can I go without working full time and give up the income in order to remain a student or, if I am out, to return to college?
- What do I want my life to be like a few years after completing the degree?

Now read over your answers. Think about them.

If you have the drive, the time and the resources to invest and want to do it, then you are ready to go. As you build toward your future success, you can make your graduate school experience truly a good one. The following chapters will show you how.

2

GETTING INFORMATION

> *After working in an office for three years, I knew I didn't want to spend the rest of my life there. I wanted to do something that would make a difference. I began to think about going to graduate school, but I didn't know how to begin. It wasn't easy to find out how to go about it. I went to the library, got on the Internet, talked to people, and then I found this great program in social work that I enrolled in. I love it.*
>
> *—LOUISA*

WHEN YOU DECIDE that graduate education is the way to the life you want, what then? Graduate education is specialized. It's important to know not only the general overall reputation of a school but the standing of the program, what it emphasizes, and, most important, the reputation of the faculty.

Begin to gather information in plenty of time. Your finished applications, with all the supporting letters, references, and other materials, may have to be submitted more than six months before you enroll. Get started on gathering information a year before you plan to begin school. For some programs you will have to start quite a bit earlier.

If you are a college student now, getting information will be easier than if you graduated years ago. You have counselors and libraries, and you can talk to professors and fellow students. But even if you are out of school, it won't be difficult if you follow the advice in this chapter.

WHERE TO FIND INFORMATION

THE INTERNET

Whether you are in college now or not, the Internet is a great source. Most universities have addresses on the Internet. This is the fastest way to get summary information. Find a computer with Internet access and a web browser program.

From some postings you will learn a lot. Sometimes virtually the entire university catalog is on line. From others you will get little more than an address to write to, though the amount of information on the web is increasing rapidly. Web pages, by and large, are put there by the administrators of that department, program, or university, and often include facts on admission, tuition costs, financial aid, degrees awarded with requirements, and a list of the faculty with information on their specialties, though the information is often mainly for undergraduates. There may be a request you can fill out at your computer to ask for more information. This goes by e-mail to the program office, and you will get their standard packet in the mail.

But there are huge differences in what each program posts. Any department at a university can put whatever it wants to on the net. The information is not in a standard form; there is no criterion for what is posted, and there is no impartial checking. Also, information may not be current. Look for a line on the page that tells when it was last updated, or look for dates throughout it.

HOW TO SEARCH THE INTERNET

Once you are online, there are two ways of searching. You can use a directory or a search engine. Among the directories are Galaxie, Infoseek, Yahoo!, and Lycos. In each of them you are presented with a set of categories; clicking on one of them leads you to a set of subcategories. You continue in this way until you find what you are seeking. The results you get with a directory depend on the topics included, the way they are classified, and the number of sites in the directory.

Search engines are huge indexes of web sites that you search using key words. To use one, you type in key words, such as university graduate physics to find programs offering advanced degrees in physics.

It takes some practice to find the sites you want, and it's not always clear that you have found everything you need. Different search engines have different rules about the use of key words. Generally, if you type "university english" every index entry in which the phrase appears exactly as typed will turn up. If you search for university AND english every entry that contains both words will appear, while if you search for university OR english you will get every entry containing one *or* both of the words. Before using a search engine, look for its rules on its web site.

The success of your search depends on the people who compile the directories and indexes, and there is a lot of variation. Early in 1998 the authors searched for lists of schools of architecture. Using directories, under education and then fields of study, we found using Yahoo! lists included 163 programs, many of them foreign. In Excite we found lists from 1994–95 of 46 bachelors and 42 master's architecture programs in the United States. Infoseek had a good list of 118 accredited U.S. architecture programs.

Some fields are much easier to search than others. It's not hard to find lists of all the accredited schools of law or medicine; these are organized professions. For business schools the Internet address http://www.gmat.org will get you a lot of M.B.A. and Graduate Management Admission Test (GMAT) planning information, and a school search database. This is a very good search facility for prospective M.B.A. students. Almost every program has a site with a wealth of information.

For law schools an excellent source is the Law School Admission Council at http://www.lsac.org. For medical schools the Association of American Medical Colleges has a site at http://www.aamc.org.

BOOKS, BROCHURES, CATALOGS

The library is a major source of information. At either a college or public library you will find directories and guides that list most universities in the United States and Canada that give graduate or professional degrees. These books describe briefly the research facilities, libraries, computer networks, tuition and fees, and financial aid. They may even list the faculty in each program.

Some are general and cover all fields. Others are much more restricted and confine themselves to specific areas. A selection of these books is listed in the References at the end of this book.

A massive six-volume set of reference books that you should find in the library is *Peterson's Guide to Graduate and Professional Programs*. This work contains descriptions of just about every program. The basic information is contained in a single paragraph, but programs that want to pay over $1,000 can prepare a rather full description which is then published in *Peterson's Guide* in a standard two-page format. Don't rely only on the two-page descriptions to find out about all graduate programs, because many good departments don't pay to put theirs in. And when you zero in on what you want and contact the program, any graduate department will send you masses of information.

We have already mentioned the Law School Admission Council. The council publishes *The Official Guide to U.S. Law Schools*. This contains information on all 179 American Bar Association-approved schools, but does not provide information on the 35 schools that are currently not approved. You may have a good reason for attending one of them, such as its location. If so, you should get information directly from the school. A list of all law schools, including the nonapproved ones, can be found in the *Law School Admission Test (LSAT) Registration and Information Book*, published annually by the LSAC. *Barron's Guide to Law Schools* also lists the nonapproved ones, and discusses the reasons you might want to attend one.

For medical schools, the American Association of Medical Colleges publishes the book *Medical School Admission Requirements* annually. It contains information on curriculum features, current first-year expenses, selection factors, and financial aid information, as well as admission requirements.

CONTACT THE PROGRAMS DIRECTLY

You need some information that you can get only through the universities themselves. Write or e-mail directly to the programs you are interested in and ask for application forms and information for prospective graduate students. For the cost of a stamp, phone call, or on-line time, you will receive a brochure telling about courses, professors, costs, and financial aid, as well as an application form.

Don't limit yourself to a narrow group of schools, but contact a broad range of programs. Your request doesn't commit you to anything.

Start early. Catalogs are published at different times of the year, depending on the university. And popular programs, such as computer science at universities famous for those departments, may run out of registration materials. You want to be sure that your request doesn't arrive so late that there is nothing left to send you.

How much material you get depends on the program. Some will inundate you with information and glossy brochures; others will send you the minimum. A program's response tells you something about how much effort the program puts into recruiting. It doesn't tell you much about the quality of the program, but it may give you an idea of the program's general attitude toward graduate students.

If you are interested in more than one department in a university, send a separate request to each. The faculty members of the department are the people who decide which applicants to admit and which ones to reject. If you are interested in landscape architecture at the University of Michigan, write to the Department of Landscape Architecture, not to the university.

Do not write to a professor to ask for an application form. The professor won't have it, probably won't know how to get it, and may just put your letter to one side, planning to take care of it later. This may or may not happen and could mean a long delay. It's not that professors don't care or that they are absentminded. Their job is to be professors, not admissions administrators.

CONTRAST AND COMPARE

When you receive the brochures, read them carefully. They contain basic information that the department thinks you need to make a choice, such as the courses it offers and degree requirements. The materials tell you something about the program. Is it clear and well written? Do the people appear to want enthusiastic students, or is it a bare recital of facts? Try to look at all the information you get with a critical eye.

If you want to learn more about a particular locality and the facilities available in that area, you can write to the university admissions office and ask for *undergraduate* admission materials. Often the material for undergraduates tells you more about the town or city and its surroundings.

CATALOGS AND CLASS SCHEDULES

Every university has a full catalog listing all the departments, programs, and degree requirements; it can be a book-length document. Some are sent free, but at other universities the applicant may be charged a few dollars. Even if there is a small cost, it may be worthwhile to pay it and get these catalogs, particularly if you are undecided. They will give you a better picture of the whole university. If you are interested in English, for instance, you may also want to know what courses are offered in related fields such as comparative literature and linguistics.

Usually the catalog lists all the graduate courses offered by your department. But beware, the courses on the list may not be scheduled very often. See if you can get a schedule or timetable that gives the courses offered in the current year. Even more informative is a list of the classes not only offered, but actually taught during the last couple of years. If you ask the department secretary, he or she may send it to you. Keep in mind that a course may have been offered but not actually given. If there was not much student interest, or the professor suddenly changed plans, the course may have been canceled. If it is rarely given, or repeatedly canceled, it is a sign that something may be wrong. The professor may be a bad teacher, or unable to attract students to the area.

IF YOU ARE A STUDENT NOW

If you are a student, you can either choose to go straight on to graduate study or, if you are not certain, you can take a year or two off to work. Your big decision will be what area to study, because in graduate school you specialize from the start. You may want to keep on, learning more about what you have been doing, or you might want to make a change. You are choosing a career path, not just a field of study.

Get to know your current professors. You will need good recommendations. Show the faculty members whom you will ask for references that you are a strong student and are interested in the subject. Get good grades in their classes. Work on the assignments and hand them in promptly so the instructor can read your papers over without pressure. And go to see the professor during office hours. Since you are considering this field for your life work, you should be interested in it. If you don't have questions to ask and topics to discuss, maybe you should think about some other field.

There are many things you can do to get good references. Chapter 7 deals with them in detail.

A CHANGE IN UNIVERSITIES IS GOOD

Unless you have a good reason for staying at your undergraduate school, you should plan to change universities when you start graduate study. It looks better on your record if you have done well at more than one school. You already know your current teachers, and you should get exposed to different points of view. Your department, even if it is large, may have an orientation—a kind of group outlook on the field. When you change schools, you will meet new people and new ideas.

Maybe your department thinks you are great and will make you a fine offer of financial aid to keep you as a graduate student, but think about leaving anyway. Don't let inertia make the choice for you. If you have a good offer from one place, you can probably get similar offers from similar schools. If you can't, perhaps you should stay, but be aware that something might be wrong if no similar department thinks you are that good. It is possible that you are truly an exceptional undergraduate student at a school with little prestige. If you think you have the ability to become a leader in the field, go for the best program possible even if the financial aid is much less. You will see how this helps when it comes time to start your career.

If you are at a university with a graduate or professional program, even if you do not plan to stay there for graduate work, talk to the faculty in your chosen field. Ask your instructors which universities have strong departments and the names of good researchers in them. Professors want their students to succeed, and they will usually have a clear idea which programs are the best and the best for you.

There is probably an office at your college where you can get information on different universities and the programs they offer, as well as on fellowships and financial aid.

The Graduate Adviser in your own department (or, if you are going into a new field, the adviser in that department) can give you a lot of information even if you plan to go to another university. This faculty member is in general charge of the academic progress of graduate students and will know a lot about different programs. He or she may send you to professors who have good information about the area of your interest. You can find out how, or whether, you would fit into the graduate program at your own university. The Graduate Adviser also has a big say in who gets admitted to the program, can estimate your chances of getting financial support, and also can suggest programs that suit your interests and abilities.

IF YOUR COLLEGE IS SMALL

If you are a student at a college that has no graduate program in your field, you probably know the faculty members better than you would at a large university. Ask their opinion, describe your goals;

be as honest as you can. This is the time to get advice based on your real abilities and interests.

Faculty members will often recommend the school where they were graduate students, but you have to take this advice with a grain of salt. For many people, graduate school was a good time in their lives, and their alma mater may have acquired a golden glow. You might ask if the faculty member sent other students to his or her university, and what happened to them. If this professor has recommended several students who were successful, the recommendation should carry a lot of weight. And you can contact those students and ask about their experiences. Information of this kind, from people with an educational background similar to yours, can be valuable.

NOT A STUDENT NOW?

Students returning after being out of school for some years have gained valuable experience, maturity, and perspective. However, with the ties to your undergraduate college weakened by time, it can be more difficult to get the necessary information. Don't give up hope. There are ways to find out what you need to know.

VISIT A NEARBY UNIVERSITY

If a university near you has a department in your area, go there and talk to the professor in charge of admissions in your field, even if you don't plan to apply there. That faculty member, the one who recruits new graduate students, can give you a wealth of information and can tell you how you would fit into their program. Also ask for the names and office hours of other faculty members who are working in that field. Many faculty members are willing to discuss their area with a prospective student. Some may not want to be bothered, but most will be delighted.

If you are not well suited to this university, the recruiting faculty member might suggest other programs that would be better for you.

FINDING LEADERS IN THE FIELD

A university library will have some things that are not in most public libraries. There you can probably browse through professional and scholarly journals in the fields that interest you. Often the current issues of these periodicals are on open shelves in a subdivision of the library devoted to the field. Note the authors of the articles, and the names that appear in bibliographies or lists of references, particularly if some occur repeatedly. You may not be able to understand clearly what is written, but you will see who is publishing or on editorial boards of the journals and you will get a general idea of the work that these authors are doing and can see how their interests match yours.

If you find yourself influenced by a book or an article, consider the university where the author teaches. There you would have a chance of working with that person.

A university will often have catalogs from other universities. You can identify some of the faculty at those other universities and find out what they have published and where. Look on the Internet or in *Who's Who in America* or in similar books. *Who's Who in American Education* gives information on eminent people in the field of education, so you can learn where someone has worked and where he or she went to school.

LEARN FROM THOSE WHO KNOW

And even while you are looking at the Internet and publications, talk to people in the field. The more you learn about the field, the clearer your own ideas will become. Really listen to what they have to say. You may choose to specialize in a different area of the field, or completely change your mind. Perhaps you are planning to go to medical school. Your choice of a specialty will be made later, but family practice appeals to you. Try to find a specialist in family practice to talk to, but even an orthopedic surgeon will have valuable information. You may change your mind after getting a new point of view.

Get as many opinions as possible. Take anything that you are told and think it over, evaluating what each person tells you. What some people say will be worthwhile, what others say won't be; they may contradict or conflict with each other. Someone who studied at one institution years ago may look back with fond nostalgia and rate that school more highly than other people would; the school may no longer be as good as the old graduate remembers. Recent alumni can tell you more about what it is actually like now.

Contact your own undergraduate school and talk to professors there and other alumni who would know. Most people do not mind giving advice; in fact, they may be flattered to be asked. You may have noticed that many people enjoy talking about their own life experiences.

Ask them what other sources of information you can look at and to whom you can speak. It is particularly helpful if someone can recommend a faculty member at a school you are considering.

The more you know, the better chance you have of choosing the right program for you.

CHAPTER 3

DECIDING
WHERE TO APPLY

> *I sent for information from about a dozen different graduate schools and then I began to get masses of material from them. Almost all of the programs sounded so great it was hard to evaluate them. How could I tell which really would be the best for me? At first I didn't even know what I should look for.*
>
> *—ELLIOT*

DECIDING WHERE TO apply for admission is a big step. While the brochures are free, sending in your applications is not. When you send in your application, you will have to include an application fee. The costs vary, depending on the university, but it may be $40 or as much as $60. If you receive many glossy booklets and catalogs from different schools, each describing its program in glowing detail, how do you know which ones offer programs that will be good for you?

WHAT TO LOOK FOR

FIRST, THE FACULTY

What is most important in graduate school is the quality of the department and the faculty with whom you will work. They are the people who admit you, who watch over your progress, who will have a big influence on whether you get the financial aid that will enable you to afford your education, and who help you to shape your future career. The faculty are the ones who make or break a graduate program.

It is important to study with people who are respected and known in the field. You want to find out who the faculty are, their academic degrees, what research they have done, and how their interests match yours, and also the ratio of faculty to students. A good brochure will contain much of this information.

Of course, faculty members don't always stay in one place. Some leave the department for other universities, some retire, but even if a few professors move away, a good department usually stays good. Unfortunately, mediocre departments don't change much either.

Your fellow students will be important to you, but they are attracted by the reputation of the faculty and should match its quality.

In a professional field, you will want to find out about the faculty members' experiences away from the university. Have the law professors worked as practicing attorneys? Are the medical school professors currently working as doctors? Is the program associated with a first-rate hospital?

Besides the quality of the faculty, there are other things you have to find out in order to make a wise decision. (Costs and financial aid are dealt with in Chapter 4.) You should know:

- whether you have the requirements to be admitted,
- how long it will take to get the degree,
- how the program is ranked,
- whether it is accredited,
- how the graduates do on professional exams,
- what percentage of graduates of the program get jobs in the field, and
- what your prospects are for getting financial aid.

THE REQUIREMENTS YOU MUST SATISFY

The brochures will give you an idea of how selective the programs are in terms of the grade point average and test scores required. It's a good idea to apply to programs that are roughly at your own level, measured by your grades, your GRE or other tests, and your academic record. If you graduated from a college that is not well known, or if your grades or test scores are not stellar, you probably won't be admitted to the highest-ranked programs. The professors may be right or they may be wrong, but most of them have an idea of which undergraduate bachelor's degrees are the "best," and they want students from those colleges. If you do not fit their profile, they will probably not accept you.

Do you have the undergraduate grades you need? A university may specify that on a scale where A equals 4.0, to be considered for admission you will need a 3.0 or a 3.5 average from your undergraduate work. If your grades are lower, your chances are not good. And even if your grade point average meets the minimum, programs that have lots of applicants may not accept you. Schools often set their minimums unrealistically low; most of their applicants will have a much higher average, and they are usually the ones accepted.

If you have special circumstances, you can contact the Graduate Adviser, explain what they are, and ask that you be considered. But usually if higher grades than you have are required, particularly at a program that gets many applicants, it is a waste of time to apply there. Also, don't bother to apply, even as insurance, to a school that you would not want to go to.

The brochures will tell you which graduate examination scores you must submit. If the Graduate Record Examination (GRE) is required, is it just the general examination, or do you also have to take a specialized subject exam?

Professional programs have specific examinations. The three major exams are the Graduate Management Admission Test (GMAT) for a degree in business administration, the Medical College Admission Test (MCAT), and the Law School Admissions Test (LSAT), but tests also exist for dental, veterinary, and pharmacy students, as well as others. One of the most important reasons for starting the application process early is that you will need time to prepare for and take these exams, and to have your scores sent directly to the departments. You can get books and take courses to help you with these tests. (See Chapter 8.)

HOW MANY YEARS TO THE DEGREE?

How long will it take to get the degree, and what course work is required to get it? The information sent by the department should give you a clear idea of the time needed for a master's degree, and of the requirements for a doctorate. The master's will usually take from one to three years, depending on the field, and will have specific requirements in terms of courses, credits, and possibly a thesis. The thesis will be a substantial project, but nowhere near the length and difficulty of a doctoral thesis.

The Ph.D. will take longer, and the department should be able to tell you the average length of time to the degree, and the dropout rate. The time required for a Ph.D. depends largely on the area of study. In *Pursuit of the Ph.D.*, by Bowen and Rudenstine (1992), the median time for a Ph.D. in history is given as 8.3 years, in the sciences as 6.1 years. But there can be major differences in the same field from one university to another.

The time it takes different doctoral students also varies. Some are in a hurry, and try to finish as soon as possible. Others enjoy the graduate student life and take their time. A few drift along with no sense of urgency. Some of these eventually get their degrees; others can be seen living a semi-student life in the corners of university towns.

Ph.D. recipients from schools in the top quarter in the 1995 National Research Council study took less time than the average to get their doctorates. There are various possible explanations for this. One is that graduate students in the top schools spend less time earning money by teaching—more of them are supported by fellowships or other funds. Or perhaps students in the programs in the top quarter are better prepared, or can do the work faster.

Almost every graduate faculty member thinks that it now takes too long to get a doctorate. Many programs try to push students through faster than they used to; some succeed while other programs don't really work at it.

A dropout rate of 50 percent in some Ph.D. programs is not

unusual, but again it depends on the field and the program. This is not as bad as it sounds. Before starting work on a doctorate, students don't know what it is going to be like. Quite a few of them find that they don't really want to do this, and stop with a master's degree. This is a very reasonable thing to do and does not reflect badly on the student or the program. And they end up with a master's, which can give them a jump-start in their careers.

RANKINGS OF PROGRAMS

You can find guides to specific programs which cover one field in depth, books on medical schools, law schools, M.B.A. programs, and so forth. Many of them also rank the various programs. Some of these are in libraries. Others are for sale in every large bookstore. Books that rank graduate programs are listed in the References section at the back of this book.

In 1995 the National Research Council published what is probably the most authoritative and complete ranking available. In 1993 thousands of faculty members throughout the country were asked to rate different programs in their fields. Each one filled out questionnaires rating 50 programs (chosen at random for each rater). In the 41 fields that were surveyed, more than 100 ratings were obtained for each of the 3,564 programs.

The survey measured the scholarly quality of the faculty and the effectiveness of the program in educating research scholars and scientists. A condensed version was published as *Student Guide to Research-Doctorate Programs,* National Research Council, 1996.

There was a strong similarity in the ratings of the 1,916 programs that were rated both in this study and in a 1982 study that covered many of the same programs.

But you should be aware that many informed people question the value of these rankings. A department head in history might be asked to rate the history Ph.D. programs in fifty different universities. In half of them he doesn't know a soul in the department, so his opinions, if he gives them, are pretty shaky.

Still, the rankings measure in a rough way the prestige of the departments. Other guides, such as U.S. News's *Best Graduate Schools*, also rank programs by field. This report is published annually, and one issue each year of the magazine has much information on the subject. These rankings are also questioned. The Association of American Law Schools and the American Bar Association said that the 1996 U.S. News rankings of law schools were "conceptually flawed and misleading to consumers."

Highly ranked programs have better-known faculty. After all, that's a major reason for their high ranking. If you hope for an academic job, the more well known and respected your adviser is, the more it will help you get a job. And if your goal is a career in business, a Master's in Business Administration from a highly rated school will almost certainly get you a better job with a higher salary than if you go to a school with a lower ranking.

But if you are a high school teacher whose salary will automatically go up if you earn a master's degree, the only point in going to a demanding school is the presumably higher quality of your education. It is the degree after your name that counts, not the university's reputation. Some public and private schools even raise salaries as the teachers get additional credits during the time they work toward their graduate degrees.

Sometimes a department is not highly ranked as a whole, but still has the best faculty in the area that interests you. And you may get more time and attention from the faculty if they are not whizzing around the world on glamorous fellowships. Or, a small program may be very good in some subfields, but may not offer much choice. If you have a clear idea of what you want to do, look for specialists who can tell you about the best programs.

ACCREDITATION

Is a program accredited? Accreditation is important in some professions, and crucial in many, such as medicine or law. If you want to be a lawyer, in some states you must have a degree from an accredited law school to take the bar exam. It is the same for other professional schools. A school that is not accredited will probably not volunteer that information. You will have to find out for yourself.

There are two kinds of accreditation: institutional and programmatic. For the first kind, there are six regional associations that accredit universities and colleges as a whole in their regions. The addresses of these associations are given in the back of this book.

For the second kind, there are thirty-five specialized agencies that accredit programs in their specialties; for example, the American Medical Association and the American Association of Medical Colleges jointly accredit Doctor of Medicine programs.

Both the American Medical Association and the American Bar Association are widely known and respected accrediting bodies. If you search for "AAMC" (American Association of Medical Colleges) on the Internet, you will find a page called "About the AAMC." Here you will find a list of all accredited U.S. and Canadian medical colleges.

For law schools, get the *LSAT & LSDAS* (Law School Data Assembly Service) *Registration and Information Book* published annually by the Law School Admission Council. This is the free book you will need to register for the LSAT. It contains lists of U.S. law schools approved by the American Bar Association, and also of schools not approved by the ABA.

The LSAC says "American Bar Association approval enables a school's graduates to satisfy the legal education requirements for admission to the bar in all jurisdictions in the U.S. Graduation from an unapproved law school may qualify a person to take the bar examination in the state in which the school is located, but generally does not qualify the person for the bar examination in other states." As of this writing, 179 law schools were approved and 35 were unapproved. You should check recent information. If you are interested in an unapproved school, find out if it recently has received approval.

The Association of Collegiate Business Schools and Programs accredits M.B.A. programs. Reputable business schools are careful to have their programs accredited. If you are unsure about the accreditation of a business school, contact the ACBSP directly.

Every well-known university will have its programs accredited. At one time the University of Illinois had a small program that did not get accreditation because it did not have a sufficient number of faculty. There was not enough student demand to justify hiring more professors and increasing the size of the program. The university abolished the program rather than continue to offer one that was unaccredited.

If you are thinking about an obscure university or a little-known program, you should be concerned about accreditation. Ask the program for a written statement on its accreditation status. If you ask, they must give it to you. Another way to get the information is to ask the relevant agency that keeps track of accreditations.

PROFESSIONAL EXAMINATIONS

When you finish your graduate program, will you need to take a professional examination? If so, will it be administered nationally, or by the state as the bar examination is for lawyers? If you attend a law school in the state where you intend to practice, you will take classes taught by professors qualified to practice law in that state; this can be a great help in preparing you for the bar exam. You will also probably take a postgraduate course specifically to prepare you to pass the exam.

On the other hand, if you are choosing actuarial science, the sequence of examinations is given by the Society of Actuaries, a national organization, not by the state, so you can work in any state. The society gives a complicated and difficult sequence of courses and examinations that enable you to become an Associate of the Society. You have to pass these examinations in order to succeed in the field.

For each department you're investigating, you should try to find out how many graduates pass these exams. Departments may not know these numbers, since some of their graduates will take these tests without telling their schools. But people who run a good program will tell you what they know. If you try to get this information and the department won't help you, be wary.

WHAT ABOUT JOBS?

Where are a school's graduates working, and what kinds of salaries are they earning? This information may not be easy to find out. Graduate faculty want bright, talented applicants, and their official literature will state every fact in the best possible way and not include anything that might discourage a prospective student.

Talk to people to find out about employment opportunities. Current graduate students will have a wealth of information, and rumors, about the current job situation. The best way to find students is to visit the university. (See the section below on making a visit.)

It's harder to find former students. Current students can give you the names and locations of friends who have recently graduated. The program itself may give you the names of some, but won't give you the name of anyone who disliked it, or who failed. Still, as you keep collecting information you will build up a list of people who know something about the program.

What are your chances of getting the job you want? You might discover that only about 20 percent of the Ph.D. graduates in history from a particular university find employment as history professors. If you are set on being a history professor, is getting a Ph.D. in history from that university worth the effort and expenditure it will take? Should you even apply, or should you try for more prestigious schools whose history doctorates have a better employment record?

Maybe you think this is the best program that will admit you, you love history enough, and are willing to take the chance that you will be that one in five. Only you can make the decision. After all, good people are needed in every field. If that is your goal, aim for an academic job but remain flexible so that your degree can be used in another position, like Hal, who has a Ph.D. in history and was hired to write histories of the national parks.

Or maybe you decide to think it over and see if there is another field that interests you in which you'd have better career opportunities.

When she heard how small her chance would be of getting work as a historian, Flora, who was interested in social history, decided to work on a doctorate in sociology and ended up specializing in demography. She now has a high-level position in the United States Census Bureau that she loves.

WHAT IS THE CHANCE OF FINANCIAL AID FROM THE PROGRAM?

Before you apply, you don't know whether you will be offered financial aid by the program, in the form of a fellowship, teaching assistantship, tuition waiver, or some combination of those. However, the recruiting materials will give you some idea of the proportion of their students, at the master's and the doctoral level, who get financial aid. By far the largest source of funds for most students is the university they are attending. Financial aid includes assistantships for which you have to work; these are a great way to solve at least half of your financial problems. The programs may give some numbers, such as percentages of master's and doctoral students who receive financial aid from them, but they may not be very specific about the amount of the aid.

They have funds at their disposal to attract students, but generally they won't allocate them until all the applications are in and they can make comparisons. Read their brochures very carefully on this point. If you can't find much useful information, you can telephone. The material you receive will contain the name of the faculty member, probably the Graduate Adviser, who does the recruiting. Call, and say frankly that you can't enroll as a graduate student without financial aid. Ask what your chances are. What you want to know is, of all the applicants accepted by the program, what proportion are offered financial aid amounting to half or more of their total expenses: tuition, fees and living expenses.

The information you get may be vague, but you can compare programs on the basis of what you learn.

OTHER CONSIDERATIONS

Does the university publish a journal in your program? If so, that's a strong indication that it is a good department, and the faculty members who are editors are respected and recognized in their field.

What about the library? If you are interested in engineering, does the engineering school have its own library with many volumes and periodicals, or are the engineering books a small part of the campus library?

Another aspect of highly ranked schools is that the students are usually "better." They may not be any smarter, but they are used to a high level of competition. Many of them have come from rigorous undergraduate schools and are well prepared for a demanding graduate program. Students who come from an easygoing liberal arts school or an undemanding state university to a first-rate research program are often taken aback by the amount and quality of work required and the sometimes aggressive competition.

At one university the program may be strictly prescribed; at another the students may have more freedom. You will have to think about what is best for you.

You may be tempted to apply to a program that you are just about certain to get into, even though you don't really want to go there. Imagine that you have just received an acceptance from that university. If your first reaction would be disappointment, don't apply.

The Graduate Adviser at any good program can make a quick judgment of the level that you should be considering.

To sum up, the criteria that are important are:

- reputation of the faculty,
- breadth and depth of class offerings,
- required examinations,
- average time to degree,
- employment success of graduates,
- selectivity of the program,

- library, computer and other facilities,
- journals in your field published by the university.

EVALUATE AND DECIDE

Books, guides, and the Internet are a start, but what they can tell you is limited. You need more information to find the right program. How do you get it? Talk to people; ask anyone who knows the field which are the best graduate programs. If you are interested in becoming a doctor, see if a physician you respect can give you an opinion on medical schools. Or if you are interested in architecture, try to find an architect who will give you his evaluation of architectural schools. One school of architecture may be known for its wild and crazy creativity, while another specializes in structural design. If it is an academic field like philosophy or musicology, then ask professors who are teaching those subjects. People don't mind being asked—everyone likes to be consulted as an expert.

VISIT IF YOU CAN

It is a good idea to visit the universities that are on your short list. There are three times you might do this: before you apply, after you apply but before you have heard the result, and after you have been accepted. If you are fairly sure that you will be accepted, you can visit between application and acceptance, but you are risking a wasted trip if you are rejected or offered little financial aid. On the other hand, if you are a promising applicant the department is more likely to help you with travel expenses during this period. Visiting after you are accepted is dealt with in Chapter 9. If you have the time and money to visit a university before you are accepted, you can look over the town and the program while making a good impression on the faculty. Contact the recruiting faculty member and make an appointment to visit. While you are at it, ask if the department will pay your travel expenses, or at least some of them. Departments are used to this sort of request, and if you are a promising applicant they will try to help you. If you have not yet applied, tell them that you are very interested in the program and mention a few points in your favor. The help can range all the way from nothing, to a spare bed somewhere, to a fully paid trip.

Don't go without an appointment. Your visit will be much more productive if the faculty members know you are coming; it's annoying to a busy person to have an applicant suddenly appear wanting time and attention right away.

The easiest way to arrange your visit is by telephone. When you call, and get to the right person, take a little time spelling out your name and giving a few facts about yourself. If you have already applied, give the recruiter time to remember your file, or maybe to look you up on a database of applicants. You want to arrange a date for the visit and an appointment with the Graduate Adviser or other faculty recruiter. Tell them that you also want to talk to some current graduate students. If you already know the field you are interested in, ask if you can talk to a faculty member in that area.

WHAT YOU SHOULD DO ON YOUR VISIT

You want to see the physical setup of the program—its offices, library, laboratories, and other facilities. You want to see the town, and the area around campus where you might be living. You should check out prices, particularly for housing. Buy a copy of a local newspaper and look at the rental housing want ads. If the school has a student newspaper, get a copy of that. Pick up a copy of every free flyer that you are offered.

But most of all, you want to talk to people. The recruiter will give you a fairly standard explanation of the program—you are not the first person to visit. You may also have appointments with graduate students and faculty members. These can be very valuable, as you will get a good idea of whether you will like the place, and how you will fit in.

Prepare yourself with a list of questions and topics you want to talk about. It will save time and make a better impression if you don't ask questions that are answered in the information you already have from the program. One of your questions for the re-cruiting faculty member should be about your chances for financial aid.

The students and faculty you see by appointment will be more or less prepared for your visit. They want to give you a good impression, but they are by no means professional recruiters. Sometimes they will be quite frank about the program, and your prospects in it, for good or ill. You can ask the graduate students about the faculty, how many of them are approachable and whether they treat the students well. However, you should also try to talk to people who are not on your appointment list.

Find out where the graduate student offices are in the department. They are usually the ones with several names listed on the door. Walk in and start talking to any likely-looking person. When you say that you are a prospective graduate student, most current students will be glad to talk to you. People like to talk about their lives, and to give advice. But remember, one student who loves the place or hates it may be an eccentric. You will have to talk to several.

Ask about the general atmosphere in the department. Are the people there remote, friendly, highly competitive? When something goes wrong, are the administrators accessible? Do they have coffee hours, and if they do, is there conversation between faculty and students, or do faculty members only talk to people they already know?

The visit is important in another way. When you visit a school, you want to show that you are a serious person with the potential to do well.

Kenneth, an older student who had had a variety of jobs in the ten years since receiving his B.A., applied to seven programs. He only visited one, the University of Illinois at Urbana-Champaign, where he talked to several professors who specialized in American history. He must have made a good impression. Of the wide range of schools he applied to, UIUC was the only school that admitted him with some financial aid.

A WARNING TO SCIENCE STUDENTS

In laboratory sciences such as chemistry, new graduate students are often assigned to a potential thesis adviser at the time they enter, or very shortly thereafter. You may be offered a research assistantship in some professor's lab, and from there it is a natural progression to specializing in that area and writing a thesis under his or her direction. The initial assistantship may determine the course of your professional life, as it can be difficult to change advisers and labs. Since it is crucial for you to get a good adviser, you should try to be assigned to someone you have chosen, rather than taking your chances.

In order to make a good choice, you have to know the strengths of the faculty and which professor would be the best for you. It is worth spending time on this effort by talking to people who know, including current graduate students. If you are entering a program with this sort of setup, try to get as much information as you can about the faculty before you have to decide.

If you are able to visit the university, you are in a much better position to get this information. Ask to be assigned to the faculty member who is best for you.

WHAT IS YOUR GOAL?

As you are collecting information, keep thinking about your goals. When you learn more about what programs are available, you may change your mind about what you really want to do. Sometimes your ideas shift. Joe's did.

Joe had a B.S. in civil engineering, but after working for four years as an engineer in Latin America and observing the poor health of many of the people, he began to get interested in biological sciences and thought of combining that with engineering. He decided to apply to Brown University to work on a Ph.D. in bioengineering.

When he visited the department and talked to the people there, he found out that engineering was emphasized, not biology. He realized he was more interested in what the physiology graduate students and faculty were working on than in what the bioengineers were doing. So he applied, was admitted, and got his Ph.D. in physiology. Now he is teaching in a small college that does not have a big budget for materials, and finds that his engineering know-how comes in handy. The college has limited funds for scientific equipment, but Joe can put together his own, and it is state-of-the-art.

THE FUTURE YOU WANT

At this point it is good to stop and take a look at your career possibilities. You have been learning about the various programs and finding out about their reputations. Now it is time to narrow your focus and think about what would be best for *you*. Compare the brochures with an eye to what you want in your education. One graduate school can be very, very different from another. See what each emphasizes.

In order to weigh your possibilities, take a piece of paper and at the top write down the field you are interested in. If you are considering more than one field, start another paper for each. Then answer these questions:

- Am I sure that this is the field for me?
- What degree do I need to work in this field?
- What are my chances of getting a job?
- Will it pay enough?
- How long will the program take?
- Is the program offered at enough institutions so I have a choice?
- Do I need an accredited program?
- Do I need to take a professional examination? If so, is it a state or a national examination?

BE REALISTIC

Start making a list of strong programs, but be realistic about your background and ability. The very best programs are extremely competitive, and you will waste time and energy in applying if you are not a truly outstanding candidate. Also, each application costs quite a bit to send in.

As you begin to make choices, don't be too quick to eliminate programs. The academic world is changing and new fields are being formed, particularly in the sciences and technology. In the humanities and liberal arts, interdisciplinary programs create new opportunities. For example, students with degrees in logic or art may find high-paying jobs working on computers. A person with a degree in teaching English may be hired to teach foreign-born experts, say Japanese bankers, to communicate in standard English.

Innovative programs can be created when two separate areas are combined. A student can now get a degree that combines business administration and computer science, or one in architecture and urban planning. Some of these programs are not widely known; you will have to ask in order to find them.

MAKING YOUR CHOICE

To help you decide where to apply, put the brochures out on a table and choose half a dozen or more programs that sound promising. Select a range, from a program that is unlikely to admit you, to one that is just about certain to accept you (as long as you want to attend it). The number you apply to will depend on how much effort you want to put in and how much money you have to spend. Melissa applied to eight programs, Max to only one, but both were successful. Max was foolish but lucky. You should probably apply to at least four; some people advise ten. But don't apply to so many schools that you cannot do a good job on each application. Take your time with this decision; it's going to have a big effect on the rest of your life.

Sending in an application can cost up to $60. If you are financially in need, some programs will let you send in your application without paying the fee. Contact them to see if you satisfy their requirements and can apply without paying.

QUESTIONS TO ANSWER

To help make up your mind where to apply, take each program you are considering; on a separate piece of paper write the name of the university at the top and then the answers to these questions:

- What degrees are given in the field?
- How high does the program rate?
- Are the faculty good?
- Are they doing what I am interested in?
- How specialized is the department?
- What are the course and thesis requirements to get my degree?
- How long will it take?
- Can I afford it?
- What are the possibilities for financial aid?
- Do I have the prerequisites for the program?
- What are my chances of being accepted?
- What are my chances of getting a job I want after I finish there?
- What is the tuition?
- Are there fees in addition?
- How much will it cost me to live there?
- Does the university have suitable graduate student housing?

Other questions you might have to consider are:

- Will I find help in getting child care?
- Will professional licensing requirements tie me to that part of the country?
- What about the expenses of moving there?

Before you mail in your application, you have a lot to think about. You will have to make decisions without knowing exactly what the results will be, to take tests, contact professors for recommendations, write essays, and choose a definite field and a range of possible universities. Sometimes you may feel like you are walking in the dark. The following chapters will take you through every step of the process.

It is important to give yourself lots of time to assemble the best application materials possible; this means not only the essay you must write as part of your application, but transcripts, letters of recommendation, and high scores on the required graduate admissions tests.

CHAPTER 4

PAYING
FOR THE DEGREE

When I was a graduate student in English we were living in poverty, particularly after the baby was born. My teaching assistantship helped, but it wasn't enough. I began getting these credit card offers and didn't resist. I ended up owing $5,000 on several different cards and wondered if I would have to drop out of school and give up my goal of being an English professor. I was rescued when Jane, my wife, got a part-time job after finding out that my mother would baby-sit for us. I also talked to the university financial-aid officer, who was a big help. With her assistance I planned out a program, I took out a student loan, paid off the credit card debt, and we managed to make ourselves cut expenses. I finished, got my Ph.D., and was hired as an assistant professor at a city university.

—DONALD

HOW CAN YOU pay for your graduate or professional education? Graduate school is not cheap. Working on a master's or a Ph.D. is expensive, and professional programs such as medical school or law school cost even more. During the years you are in school, you have to give up the income you'd earn if you were working. But lack of cash should not stop you. Help is available. It may not be easy to find the funds you need, but it can be done. In this chapter we talk about the best sources of funds, where to look, and how to tap them.

THE ESSENTIALS

The first thing to do is to examine the figures. What would your expenses be at schools you are considering?

The costs will include:

- tuition,
- fees,
- health insurance (this may be included in the fees),
- books,
- travel and local transportation, parking, auto insurance,
- computers, art supplies, or other necessary equipment,
- housing,
- entertainment (movies, cable TV, CD's, beer . . .),
- living expenses, including rent, utilities, food, clothing, telephone, etc., and
- child care, if it applies.

IN OR OUT OF STATE?

If you are going to a state university, it makes a big difference whether you are a resident in terms of the amount of tuition you are charged. At the University of California at Berkeley, an out-of-state graduate student pays almost $9,000 more a year than a Californian. If you are not from the state where you will be going to school, see if the department can tell you what you have to do to become a resident. In some states the residence requirement is a year, and you can satisfy it during your first year as a student there. In other states, time spent as a student does not count toward residence.

PLAN AHEAD

Read over the brochures of the schools that interest you.

Make a rough estimate of what your expenses might be to see how much money you will need, or how little.

- What is your financial situation?
- Do you have savings, or a family member, such as a working spouse, who will help subsidize you?
- Do you owe money now?
- How many years will the program take?

- Can you work while you are in the program?
- Are you willing to borrow in order to complete this degree?

Be realistic, and don't get discouraged.

USE THE BROCHURES TO PLAN YOUR BUDGET

The information the programs send out gives a standard budget, which tells the cost of tuition and fees at that school, and estimates the cost of books, and probably of living expenses. This will give you an idea, but there are other costs of staying alive, as summarized in the list above.

Compare the cost of living at the different locations. Living in a big city on the east or west coast may be a lot more expensive than living in a small or middle-sized university town away from high-cost areas. Another consideration that may have an impact on your finances if you are married is what kind of employment your spouse can find in the area.

The better a school's rating, the more likely its graduates are to find better jobs after they get the degree, but usually tuition will be higher, sometimes much higher. Because the program is more competitive, it will certainly be more difficult to get admitted into.

TWO SOURCES OF FUNDS

Some of your funds will come from areas that are under your control: loans, outside jobs, savings, or family. Everything else will come from one of two sources. First is internal funding, money that is controlled by the university you are attending, and second is money from external sources such as national fellowships. The first source includes fellowships, assistantships of all kinds, work-study jobs, grants, and tuition waivers. The second source, external fellowships, consists of scholarships or grants that you apply for independent of your university. We will concentrate on internal funding, since that is where most students get their money.

A great deal of financial aid is controlled by the universities, and you should make the most of this fact. There will not usually be a central location where all the financial aid possibilities are listed. It's not that easy. The places to look are first in your own department or program, then at the Financial Aid Office of the university, in the Graduate College of the university, and in the college in which your department is located. The administrative organization varies from one university to another, but generally your department will be in a college—the history department will probably be in the Liberal Arts College. In addition, there is often a Graduate College that deals with the graduate programs in the university. All of these places are possibilities, but the most important one is your own department.

FINANCIAL AID FROM YOUR PROGRAM

Since each department selects the students to receive assistantships and also many of the fellowships, start your search for funds in the departments before you apply.

Begin by reading the information that you are given. See what is available in the programs you are interested in. Look carefully at the descriptions of financial aid for students in each program. If you have questions, ask the Graduate Adviser what funding is available. He or she can tell you about assistantships and also the fellowships that the department controls, and estimate your chances of getting help.

Financial aid through your university, generally, is in the form of fellowships or scholarships, teaching assistantships, research assistantships, other assistantships, work-study programs, and student loans. Loans are not controlled by the university, but you apply for them through the Financial Aid Office.

In addition to the department, ask the university Financial Aid Office about other sources such as university-wide fellowships, assistantships, grants, work-study programs, outside jobs, and loan programs that are financed with university funds.

Some external fellowships are funded by the government or by foundations, such as the $25,000 Luce Fellowship, but these often require a nomination from your program or the university. The faculty in your department nominate and recommend the students for such fellowships. You can apply for some external fellowships independently, but to be successful you will need recommendations from your department.

Many external awards are for students in specific fields, such as the U.S. Public Health Service Fellowships for students in the biological or social sciences, or the Foreign Language and Area Studies Fellowships in such fields as Asian, African, Latin American, and Russian and East European Studies. They all have different deadlines and application forms. Books describing these sources are listed in the References section at the back of this book.

If you are now an undergraduate, don't wait until you are admitted to a graduate program. Apply directly during your senior year to the granting organization for a national fellowship. If you are qualified, your department should help you with this application.

If you come into a program with an external fellowship that does not pay tuition, you may still be granted a tuition waiver. After all, if you are awarded a good external fellowship, you are probably better qualified than a new graduate student who is a teaching assistant, and teaching assistants often get tuition waivers. A $15,000 fellowship sounds good, but $10,000 in tuition takes a very big bite out of it. It does not seem fair for a fellowship holder to have to use the fellowship funds on tuition, and be worse off than a teaching assistant who gets $10,000 plus a tuition waiver. If you have an external fellowship, be sure to ask about a tuition waiver, and don't hesitate to use this argument. The tuition waiver is so important that it should influence your choice of where to go.

A GOOD APPLICATION CAN BRING MONEY

When you send in your application for admission, you also apply for financial aid, either as part of the general application or on a separate form. A good application, with good references, transcripts, and a winning essay, can easily be worth $20,000 a year to you. A half-time assistantship may bring in $8,000 to $12,000, and tuition, except for in-state students at a public university, often exceeds $10,000 (at the University of California at Berkeley it is currently $13,378). The next chapter tells how to make your application as compelling as you can.

Some universities will automatically consider you for all fellowships, scholarships, and assistantships when you submit your application for admission. At other universities the application for financial aid is a separate form. This point should be made clear in the instructions. If the request for financial aid is separate, be sure to fill it out even if you think you will not get the money. If you don't apply, you certainly won't. Be sure to check the date the application for financial aid is due. It may be different from the date for your application for admission.

Make sure your application is as good as you can possibly make it. Be meticulous, and send it in early. Even if your qualifications are good, if your application is mediocre you may get a notice that you are accepted with no offer of financial aid.

YOUR OFFER

At the time you are accepted you may be offered financial aid, either a fellowship, teaching assistantship (TA), research assistantship (RA), some other kind of assistantship, or a combination of fellowship and assistantship, possibly with a tuition waiver. A majority of doctoral students, and some master's students, in big universities are offered some kind of financial aid. It is not at all unusual for students to be offered a waiver of tuition plus a combination of fellowships and teaching assistantships that will pay most of their living expenses. This is great, and is what most students want.

If the professors running the program think you are an outstanding student, they will make the offer as attractive as they can. They have a great deal of leeway in putting together these offers, and it is not unheard of for an applicant to bargain for a better offer.

Some fellowships are for first-year students, and are not renewable; others may be awarded for terms of several years. If you are offered a fellowship, be sure to find out for how long, or if it can be renewed or replaced by a teaching assistantship. If you are awarded an assistantship, ask if there is a cutoff time after which you get no aid. It is not likely that the department will guarantee renewal of an assistantship, but there is usually an understanding that it will be renewed for some years if your performance is satisfactory. When you know about the offers you have received (more than one, you hope), you have the pleasant task of deciding which one to accept.

TYPES OF AID

FELLOWSHIPS AND SCHOLARSHIPS

Fellowships and scholarships are cash awards, frequently given for academic excellence but sometimes on the basis of need. There is no real difference between a scholarship and a fellowship. Often an award to an undergraduate is called a scholarship and one to a graduate student is called a fellowship, but no hard and fast rule exists. Sometimes the funds are reserved for minorities or women.

You don't have to work at any specific job for the fellowship, or fulfill requirements other than keeping your grades up. It frees you to concentrate on your academic work. What you are expected to do is to make good progress toward your degree.

Fellowships usually are awarded to the most qualified students; in the case of entering students, they are ordinarily used to attract the best prospects. If you are offered a small fellowship, it may come packaged with an assistantship (see below) so that the total is a reasonable amount of money.

Departments choose which students will be offered these awards. There is tremendous variety in the amount they pay. Some fellowships with impressive names give only $500 per year; others will pay tuition and some additional cash, sometimes enough to live on, usually not. A few will pay all tuition and fees together with a generous stipend.

Fellowships usually are for a specified length of time, one to three years. Some can be renewed, but most cannot. The conditions should be explained clearly when the award is made. After a fellowship expires, the student is offered an assistantship for which teaching or other work is required.

ASSISTANTSHIPS

An assistantship usually means that you teach, or assist in research or administrative work. A *teaching assistantship* requires you either to assist a professor in class or to be responsible for a class on your own; it's a job. Though you have to work, they have many advantages, such as the teaching experience and the day-to-day contact with senior department members. Assistantships sometimes pay enough to live on.

A *research assistantship* is often in the sciences, sometimes in the social sciences, education, or liberal arts, and requires laboratory or other work under the direction of a faculty member. Research assistantships in the humanities may involve library work, construction of bibliographies, or data entry on computers and might be paid for out of the professor's research budget. Other *assistantships* require you to work in some non-teaching job, such as clerical or computer work in administration. In many universities a student can have both a fellowship, for which he or she does no extra work, and an assistantship for which there are specified duties. This is the way that a university will see that a promising student gets enough money to live on.

The amount of money, plus tuition waiver, paid by the program varies greatly from one university to another, and from one field to another. In the fall of 1996 the net value of a half-time, nine-month TA appointment in electrical engineering at one public Big Ten university was $17,232; at another it was $11,995. Much of the difference was in the tuition waiver. In English, at the same two universities, the figures were $14,858 and $10,825. At a private university, due to the tuition waiver, the net value can be as high as $28,000.

What an assistantship will involve for you is described in more detail later on in the chapter.

WORK-STUDY AND OTHER FUNDING

If you can show that you have financial need, you may be able to get a *federal work-study* job. Not every university has a work-study program, and some award these positions only to undergraduates. But many institutions include graduate students.

Up to 75 percent of the student's wages are paid by the federal work-study program. The department that employs you pays the rest. Because hiring for these positions is done by the department, people who get them usually work in areas related to their academic field, such as in university libraries, or laboratories, or assisting in summer recreation programs.

To get up-to-date information and to see if you are eligible, talk to the university's fellowship or Financial Aid Office. Work-study positions may be controlled by the department or the Graduate College, or some other entity within the university. You may have to search in order to find them.

You should also talk to the Financial Aid Office about additional funding. There are other sources, and, unless you ask, you will never find out what they are. Among them are *cooperative positions* and *internships*. Depending on what you are studying, these combine work experience in the field with your studies. These programs may be administered by a separate office or from within your department; for instance, if you are in engineering, at some schools the department will help you find out what cooperative opportunities are available in the field. You might go to school for one term and work for the company that is supporting you the next term, returning after that to your studies. Or you might be able to work in the summer and earn enough to help pay for most of the academic year.

Sometimes your employer will help with financial aid. In this case you will often have to continue working at your job.

Ted was working full time as a computer graphics artist at a small publishing firm when his boss told him he should get a master's degree and the firm would pay his tuition. Ted cut down his work hours to three-quarter time at the publishing company, went to the university and took a full class schedule in the art department, which involved many hours spent at the studio. He is still doing it and finding that it isn't easy, but so far he has not burned out.

Not every student is capable of expending all that energy. If you think you can do it, you might talk to your employer and see how much financial aid would be offered and what kind of commitment your employer would want from you after you get your degree. You might be expected to continue working for a certain specified time, or to pay back tuition if you leave your job.

ON- AND OFF-CAMPUS JOBS

Depending on your field, you may find a nonacademic job on campus that will give you experience toward your future career. Some graduate students teach not-for-credit courses in music, art, or the humanities. Students in sports medicine may coach a class of children in soccer or some other team sport. Agriculture students may tend plants in campus gardens or greenhouses.

Universities usually have centers where students find lists of off-campus jobs, an excellent source of needed cash. These may be for only a few hours, such as baby-sitting or raking leaves for a faculty family, or a real part-time position with a long-term commitment, such as working in a local hospital or for an advertising agency, which might give you good experience for what you want to do. See if you can get work that doesn't hurt your progress.

OTHER ASPECTS OF FINANCIAL AID

PRIVATE OR PUBLIC UNIVERSITIES

Highly ranked private universities often have more money to support their graduate students than public universities do, and can offer more fellowships, some of which are guaranteed for a certain number of years. If you have a strong academic record, an Ivy League school or one with similar high standards might be the place for you. But, since the private schools are smaller and have fewer undergraduates to be taught, they offer fewer teaching assistantships, and of course, their tuition is much higher than at a public university.

In the Big Ten universities as a whole, as well as other big public research universities, about 60 percent of the graduate students are supported by assistantships, many of them as teaching assistants. These assistantships usually pay barely enough to support one person, but often come with a tuition waiver. State or other public universities also have some fellowship funds, but most graduate students will have to work in an assistantship. Even with an assistantship, it is likely that you will be short of money.

In professional programs such as law, medicine, and business, teaching assistantships are very scarce; classes are usually taught by qualified professionals, not by graduate students. On the other hand, professional programs may lead to better paying work after you get the degree. (See the section below on financial aid for medical and law students.)

MASTER'S OR DOCTOR'S DEGREE?

There is a big difference in the amount of financial aid available to master's and to doctoral students. A master's is either a professional degree or, in the academic world, is considered to be an extension of the bachelor's degree. An M.A. in history will not qualify you to teach at a four-year college; only a Ph.D. will. The master's usually takes about two years, while the Ph.D. can easily take eight. The length of time varies a lot from one field to another. Doctoral degrees in the liberal arts, such as history, English, and philosophy, can take much longer than in chemistry, in which the students are pushed through fairly rapidly.

Much more financial aid is available for doctoral students. The time and effort you need for a Ph.D. is much greater. It is fairly common for a master's student to complete a degree without being granted any financial aid from the program, but rare for a doctoral student.

Faculty members are often more interested in doctoral students because that was their own path. They remember the years when they were entering the profession and had little money, and are sympathetic when others make the same choice. They are more likely to award financial aid to doctoral students partly because of this, and also because the program takes much longer. It is not reasonable to expect doctoral students to finance themselves for six or more years.

If you have a choice and are undecided about whether to work on a master's or a doctorate, apply to be admitted to the doctoral program. You'll have a much better chance of getting financial aid. If you decide later that the master's is enough schooling, you can tell the faculty and just leave. You don't owe them anything, but be sure to notify them in plenty of time so they can replace you if you have an assistantship.

FULL OR PART TIME?

Some students opt for going to school part time so they can keep on working. This is particularly true of those in some master's programs, especially if they have families to support. Sometimes it is the best solution. Two of the areas in which it is common are teaching and business administration.

But not all departments allow you to attend only part time. A lot of the professional programs won't admit part-time students. Many schools want their master's candidates in engineering to be full-time students. So do directors of most master's programs in nursing or architecture.

Some M.B.A. programs provide a path to a degree that can be taken by a person who has a full-time job. Combining school and a full-time job is difficult and involves evening and weekend classes. Still, being a part-time student is much easier in a program designed to accommodate you. These programs don't offer much financial aid, but maybe your employer will subsidize you by giving you some time off, or paying part of the tuition. If you have a good job and want an M.B.A., ask your employer about this possibility.

The definition of full-time study as a graduate student is rather elastic. Many programs say that taking four graduate courses is full time. But they only expect their teaching assistants to take three courses, two if the classes are difficult or if the teaching assignment is heavy.

If a student has an assistantship in the university administration, he or she is expected to take only two or three courses, though the work may have nothing to do with the field of study. From there it is just a step to an outside job, so your program may not object if you take two or three courses per term and tell them that you have fallen into the habit of eating three times a day. There will probably be a definition of half time, maybe taking two courses. If you fall below it, you will be treated differently by the university, because rules applying to part-time students often kick in below the half-time level.

In a regular program, part-time study has disadvantages. If you get credit for only one or two courses a term, it is going to take you years longer to get a master's degree than if you go to school full time. Many assistantships, loans, and work-study positions are given only to students who are going to school at least half time. And if you are limited to classes that meet at night or on weekends, you may miss certain courses or professors.

As for a Ph.D., most Graduate Advisers say it is almost impossible to do all the required work if you go to school part time. It would just take too many years. So you have to make a choice.

MORE ON FELLOWSHIPS AND SCHOLARSHIPS

EXTERNAL FUNDING

Many books have information on sources of external funding. Most of these give the impression that external funding is the most important source of financial aid, but this is not so. External funding can be very valuable, but for most graduate students their own university is the major source of money.

Only the most highly qualified people receive prestigious scholarships and fellowships awarded by private corporations and nonprofit organizations each year. Extremely competitive, these awards are not tied to a specific university; if you receive one, you can take it with you to any school you choose.

Examples include National Science Foundation Fellowships,

which are awarded to gifted students in one of the science or engineering fields, or the American Association of University Women's award for women graduates. There are many others. You can find more information in the References.

If you are an exceptional student you should certainly apply for some of them, particularly if you have been encouraged to do so by one of your professors. If you are now an undergraduate student, talk to your professors about external fellowships. A recommendation from a professor who is a leader carries a great weight with the committees making awards. If a well-known professor is willing to recommend you, take advantage of the offer. It wouldn't be made if the professor thought you had no chance, for the professor's own reputation is affected by the quality of the students that he or she recommends.

Most schools have Financial Aid Offices that can provide information on these and other awards. The information usually includes the amount of money to be awarded, the qualifications the applicants need, and the deadlines. If you are a senior now, ask staff members about specific awards for the program you are choosing and see if they will help you apply for these scholarships. If you are recently out of school, you can contact the people at your own undergraduate college to learn what is available.

After Helen graduated from Cornell and spent a year teaching English in China, she decided to work on a Ph.D. in Chinese history. She visited Cornell to talk to her old professor. He told her that if she applied immediately he would recommend her for a Mellon fellowship, which he thought she had an excellent chance of getting. She applied and was awarded the Mellon, which she took to Columbia. She was an attractive applicant because, with external support for three years, she did not need to be awarded any university funds.

This professor probably had had some earlier contact with the Mellon Foundation. Perhaps he had recommended students who turned out to be brilliantly successful. Whatever the reason, his recommendation meant a lot to Helen. If you are applying for one of these well-known and well-funded fellowships, a key recommendation can make the difference.

For every Mellon Fellowship, dozens more are less well known, with less funding. You will have to make a judgment as to how much work you will put into applications for external funds. Spend some time looking into these possibilities, but remember that the most important investment of your time is in the applications you send out. The programs themselves are the major source of funds.

BIZARRE SCHOLARSHIPS

Most universities have some quirky scholarships that started when some benefactor left money, say, to a redheaded left-hander studying Swahili, or to someone whose dad worked at a meat packing plant. It is worth asking at the Financial Aid Office where you can find lists of these and searching them to see if you qualify for one of these obscure fellowships. A late professor of English went all the way through Harvard to a Ph.D. on a scholarship for the most qualified person named Murphy.

These scholarships are worth checking out even though they are a long shot. If you are eligible, some of them are so specific that you won't have much competition.

MORE ON ASSISTANTSHIPS

As we have already said, most financial aid for graduate students in public universities is in the form of assistantships, awarded by the department. Teaching, research, and other assistants are part-time employees and receive a monthly salary for their work. Many universities also reduce or waive their tuition and some of the extra fees that most students are charged.

TEACHING ASSISTANTSHIPS

A university with a large number of students needs teaching assistants, particularly in fields that have many undergraduate classes, such as English or mathematics. If you plan to work on a doctoral degree in a subject taken by many students and have a superior academic record, you have a good chance of becoming a TA.

Graduate students with teaching assistantships are working part time. Because of the hours spent teaching and preparing for class, they usually take a reduced course load. But even though you may have to slow down your progress, you would be wise to become a teaching assistant. You are teaching in your field, and, as many TAs find out, once you teach a subject, you learn it so that you never forget it. If you hope to go into teaching, it gives you valuable experience and qualifications toward the day when you start to job hunt.

Besides the money it brings in, being a TA means you are part of a select group. You are a member of the department, usually with assigned office space. You have much more contact with other graduate students and faculty and will know a lot about what is happening in your department. This is important because situations in a department change and you can and should know what is going on.

A nun working on a master's in mathematics lived with church people and had no contact with other students. She never heard the department gossip and did not hear students talk about a few professors who did not finish the course syllabus but gave all students in their classes high marks. She did not realize that by chance she had taken classes with these professors; she thought she was progressing satisfactorily because her grades were all right. When she came before a committee for her oral examination, it was plain that there were great gaps in her knowledge. To her surprise and dismay she failed.

The amount of time that graduate students are expected to spend on their teaching assistantships varies, depending on the university or the department. Some TAs attend the professors' lectures and then conduct small classes based on the lectures, or supervise undergraduates' laboratory work. Others, usually the more advanced students, have charge of courses on their own, while some TAs only grade papers. Generally a TA will work from fifteen to twenty hours per week. In some ways being a TA is better than being a fellowship recipient, who gets a stipend but doesn't have the contact that comes from teaching in the department. There is tremendous variation but in many cases, counting the tuition waiver, TAs can earn as much as $20,000, which is pretty good for a half-time job. The cost of tuition that is waived is part of the income.

QUESTIONS YOU SHOULD ASK ABOUT AN ASSISTANTSHIP

Some departments award applicants sizable assistantships in order to get them to enroll, but a year or two later, after the student is well into the degree, take the assistantships away and give them to new people they want to attract. If you are offered a position as a TA, be sure to ask what are the chances that it will be renewed.

Also find out whether the assistantship pays tuition. At some schools if you get an assistantship you will have to pay for tuition from your earnings; at others the tuition is waived. Tuition costs are now so high this can make a big difference. Some universities also charge students fees as well as tuition. These are treated differently by different universities. A university may waive tuition for a teaching assistant, but require that fees be paid. And sometimes fees are high, hundreds of dollars each semester.

If a university charges fees, they are usually mandatory and cover such items as services for health care, for campus recreation, for computers, and so-called general fees that may cover the cost of campus bus service or maintaining an ice skating rink. Some universities have high fees because for legal or political reasons they want to keep the tuition low. You will have to pay attention to these two categories to avoid getting a nasty shock.

Because TAs are considered to be employees, their salaries are taxable income. However, any tuition waiver you receive is tax-free, at least for now.

Many TA salaries are paid in full over a nine- or ten-month period, and the money dries up in the summer. You can try to save 20 percent of your meager salary to tide you over the summer, but it takes superhuman self-control. There is often some teaching to be done in the summer, though less than in the academic year, and you should apply for it as soon as you can. Also, some professors have research grants that provide money for research assistants during the summer. Summer is likely to be a lean time, so try to plan for it.

Occasionally big departments do not have enough qualified graduate students to cover their undergraduate classes. They hire graduate students from other departments with the appropriate background and experience to teach their undergraduates. If your department does not award you a teaching assistantship and you have good qualifications, you can ask about teaching in other departments.

A different department that may provide a teaching job will almost always be related to your department. English and comparative literature are related, for instance. Or maybe you have a skill such as computer expertise, which can get you a job in some computer-assisted teaching program. You will have to ask around, since there is probably no central listing for these unusual positions. If you have changed your field from your undergraduate degree, you may be qualified to teach in the department of your undergraduate major.

RESEARCH ASSISTANTS

RAs receive their money for assisting faculty. A research assistantship can give you excellent academic training as well as practical experience, particularly if the research is connected with your degree and is with a professor in your area. The professor usually has a research grant from some organization, either a branch of the government or a private foundation. This grant may provide specifically for one or more research assistants. Almost always, the grant is to the university, and the funds are earmarked for the professor's research. An RA is then an employee of the university, often with salary and benefits very similar to those of a TA.

The professor with a grant will choose the students he wants as his RAs. Often they are students who have this professor as their thesis adviser, but entering students may also be offered RAs. The duties of an RA depend on the professor. There may be specific work to be done, such as helping to prepare a bibliography. An advanced student may work on one of the professor's research projects, and this work may form the basis of a thesis. Sometimes the student works closely on the faculty member's research. Other assistantships let students carry on with their own research, guided by the faculty member.

How much time a research assistantship will take depends on the faculty member. As a general rule, no student should spend more than twenty hours a week working as a research assistant, and many spend less. Even twenty hours is a lot of time, particularly if it will not help you with your course work or thesis.

Research assistantships may be awarded to entering students, but usually only in well-funded areas in engineering and science. In those fields a professor may hold various continuing grants for research, and have a team of RAs working primarily in a laboratory. Faculty members in such a department may look over the applications and choose the applicants they think are the best. They then try to get these students as their advisees.

In fields where faculty members do not ordinarily have continuing funds, RAs are rarely awarded to beginning graduate students. Usually the students have to prove that they can succeed in graduate school before being considered for a research assistantship. A faculty member in the arts or humanities may have a grant that will pay a research assistant to help with library research, or to gather data for a book. It will probably be awarded to a student who is known to have the ability or experience.

OTHER ASSISTANTSHIPS

People who have other types of assistantships work in administration, support for the university, or in special projects such as a university anniversary celebration. These assistantships, too, are usually not awarded to first-year students but go to those who are already at the institution. Some of these students are called administrative assistants or graduate associates. Ideally these assistantships are in the students' fields of interest, but some may be in administrative work. A typical job might be in computer-related work in some college office in the university.

To search for one of these positions, start at your department. If nothing is available, you will have to look further to find positions in other units of the university. Go to the college office, the graduate college office, and to the university's Financial Aid Office.

One advantage of these jobs is that they, too, may come with a tuition waiver. Also, they show a prospective employer that you are a good enough student to be supported by the university, and that you did not have to take a job delivering pizzas in dangerous neighborhoods.

Theo, a computer science whiz, had an assistantship doing programming for the university, and Max, an architectural student who had experience in building, had an assistantship supervising the department's woodshop, helping inexperienced students use the power tools to build architectural models. Max, who said that his real job was to make sure that the students left with the same number of thumbs that they came in with, got his position through his department. Neither Theo nor Max wanted academic careers when they finished their degrees, which was just as well. Their assistantships paid well but gave them no teaching experience. Theo is now a highly paid computer program designer and Max is working for a famous California architect.

If you need help in paying for room and board, and would like to live in a dormitory with undergraduates, you can apply for an assistantship in a residence hall. For performing tasks such as helping to counsel troubled students or keeping order on Saturday nights, resident assistants often get a stipend, in addition to free room and board.

WHERE TO FIND INFORMATION ON FINANCIAL AID

THE INTERNET

Even though most funding that students get comes through their schools, it is still worthwhile to search on your own. Whether you are in school or out, check the scholarship search services on the Internet. The situation is constantly changing, and you need as much up-to-date information as possible.

One search service, recommended by a number of universities, is FastWEB, which is supported by Student Services, Inc., and has information on approximately 180,000 scholarships and other financial aid programs. This is free and available on the World Wide Web. FastWEB's address is http://www.studentservices.com/fastweb/. The software will create an electronic mailbox for Student Services messages to you.

The program will ask you questions and compare your responses to the criteria for scholarships and financial aid programs. Almost immediately you'll find a list of scholarships and other awards for which you might be eligible in your mailbox. However, the list may be a bit eccentric. FastWEB may send you information that no sane person would think you need, and will probably omit some possible fund sources. You should also use the addresses below and do some searching for yourself. Additional sites are given in the Reference Addresses section at the back of this book.

An excellent Internet page called the Financial Aid Information Page is at http://www.finaid.org. It is mainly directed to undergraduates, but has a wealth of information for prospective graduate students as well.

Minority applicants should look carefully for sources of financial aid, since there are many scholarships and fellowships for minorities. Almost every university has some, but there is no central listing. Among the links, a very good source for minority applicants is the page of the Minority On-Line Information Service (MOLIS), whose address is http://www.finaid.org/finaid/focus/minority.html.

Also look at Mark's Picks, maintained by Mark Kantrowitz, the author of *The Prentice Hall Guide to Scholarships and Fellowships for Math and Science Students*, and sponsored by the National Association of Student Financial Aid Administrators. The address is http://www.finaid.org/finaid/picks.html.

LISTS IN BOOKS

Many books offer financial aid information. Some of them are listed in the References. They describe external fellowships and give the addresses so you can contact the agencies directly.

LOANS

Even with financial aid, most graduate students have to borrow some money to finance their education. This is an investment in your future that will pay dividends. But it is important to plan carefully and to make wise decisions so that you don't end up with a debt that becomes more than you can manage. Fortunately, there are several educational loans, some better for the student than others.

Before you apply for a loan, make sure that you have applied for all other forms of financial help that may be available. Financial need forces some students to drop out of school to go to work; often they don't return to get the degree. To prevent disaster, plan ahead.

FEDERAL LOAN FUNDS

The most important federal loans are called Federal Stafford Loans. Full information about them is in the booklet "The Student Guide: Financial Aid from the U.S. Department of Education, 1998–99." It is available free from the Federal Student Aid Information Center, P.O. Box 84, Washington, DC 20044. The same information is at the web site http://www.ed.gov/prog_info/SFA/StudentGuide/1996–7/sl.html#elig.

Stafford Loans come in several flavors. There are *Direct Loans* and *Federal Family Education Loan Program Loans* (called FFELP Loans), and each of these offers *subsidized* and *unsubsidized* loans. The difference between Direct and FFELP Loans is that the funds for Direct Loans come from the Department of Education, while FFELP Loan funds come from banks. This difference is not important to you as a borrower, since the terms of the loans are essentially the same. In both cases there is a fee of up to 4 percent for lending you the money, so you only get 96 percent of what you borrowed.

However, as the names imply, subsidized loans are better for you than unsubsidized loans. With a subsidized loan, you are not charged any interest and need not make any payments while you are in school more than half time, and for six months after you leave. With an unsubsidized loan, interest is charged from the day you borrow, but you do not have to start paying the loan or the interest until six months after you leave school. In both cases, after the six-month grace period you will have to start paying back the loan itself, as well as further interest that will be charged. For the unsubsidized loans, if you defer payment of the interest, that unpaid interest is added to the loan balance at the end of the grace period.

A third loan program is Federal Perkins Loans. These require exceptional financial need and, as of this writing, have a low 5 percent interest rate. You can borrow $5,000 per year up to a total of $30,000. The money is actually lent to you by the school using federal funds. Not every school uses this program. If you think you might be eligible, be sure to check the school to see if it does.

The Federal Pell Grants and PLUS loans for parents, which you may be familiar with, are only for undergraduates.

Finally, when you are finished with your education and have outstanding loans from various federal sources, you may be able to get a consolidation loan, which will convert them all into one big loan. This is a good idea, because the fewer banks and agencies you deal with, the less chance there is for error.

APPLYING FOR A LOAN

Since the financial picture keeps changing, first get up-to-date information from your university's Financial Aid Office. It is deeply involved in the loan process. The loan application, which you can get there or directly from the Department of Education, is submitted to that office, which certifies your eligibility for the loan. After you are awarded the loan, the money comes through the university, which in the case of FFELP Loans recommends to the lender when to send the money.

You will be asked to fill out an application, which must be approved by the school. If you are applying for federal aid, you will have to complete the Free Application for Federal Student Aid (FAFSA), which must be sent in and approved. The exact procedure is described in the materials accompanying the loan application forms, and depends on whether you are borrowing from a bank or directly from the federal government.

The FAFSA form is widely used, even for nongovernmental loans. Unfortunately, the form was designed for undergraduates, and some of the questions are difficult for independent students to interpret. Still, it is often required for loans from state or university sources. Many universities require, in addition, that you complete supplemental applications and also need-analysis forms. You can get any updates on other loans you could be eligible for through the Financial Aid Office.

STAFFORD LOAN LIMITS

There are limits to the amounts a graduate student can borrow in the Stafford Loan program, but they are alarmingly high. For the subsidized program, you can borrow up to $8,500 per year to a maximum of $65,000. On top of this you can get unsubsidized loans to bring your total to $18,500 per year and a grand total of $138,500. The interest rate is capped at 8.25 percent, but may be lower. With limits like these, you can get yourself into a lot of financial trouble if you are not careful.

YOU HAVE TO REPAY

It is important to emphasize that for all student loans, you do not have to graduate before the loans come due. Six months after you leave school, loan payments start to become due—even if you don't receive your degree. Once you leave school, with or without the degree, you will have to start repaying.

Currently there are several repayment plans. One has a 10-year repayment period, another allows you to repay the loan over 25 years. These are examples, and the regulations governing student loans may change. Currently, it is possible to make early payments, which can either keep the length of the loan the same and reduce subsequent monthly payments or keep the payments the same and reduce the length of the loan. When you negotiate, be sure to find out all the details from the institution that is lending the money.

Various conditions go with these loans. The loan is canceled if you die or become permanently and totally disabled. The loans are not automatically discharged in bankruptcy. Loan payments may be deferred if you re-enroll in school, are unable to find full-time employment, or have an economic hardship.

Loans are easy, almost too easy, to take out, and much harder to pay back. Repaying loans can be difficult, particularly for those going into an academic field. Even with a relatively low interest rate, not more than 8.25 percent, the cost of borrowing money is substantial. If you have a subsidized loan of $6,000 at 7 percent and pay it back over 10 years, the payments will be about $70 per month, and you will pay out a total of $8,400.

George's wife was so upset at their poverty and the decline in their standard of living when he started working on a Ph.D. in philosophy that he took out student loans, raising the amount when each of his two children were born. He finished his Ph.D. over $35,000 in debt. He got the assistant professorship he wanted at a good small school, but the tremendous debt will make their life very difficult.

If you want a career that doesn't generate a lot of money, you shouldn't start your working life with a mountainous debt to pay. You could get the job you want but spend many years paying back your student loan.

If you can do it, it is better to earn money in a job, such as a teaching assistantship, and to take out a loan only for what is absolutely necessary. It may be tempting to borrow money in order to keep the standard of living you had before going to graduate school, but you will have to pay it back with interest. It is difficult, but consider the possibility of life without a car.

NONFEDERAL LOAN FUNDS

The campus Financial Aid Office will also have information on other sources. The university may have some funds that are used for student loans. This situation will be different at each university, and you will have to ask the financial aid people to find out if there are loans available.

In a program called the Professional Education Plan, sponsored by the Educational Resources Institute, loans can be made in the range from $2,000–$20,000 per year; there is a 6 to 8 percent guarantee fee. For more information, phone the agency at 800 255-8374.

You may want to arrange a loan from a friend or family member. If you do, it is best to keep it on a completely businesslike basis. When you borrow the money, make a written statement of the amount, the interest, the schedule of repayment (for example, specified monthly payments starting six months after you leave school), and any other conditions connected with the loan. If the conditions of the loan are clear, you may avoid unpleasant arguments about money.

Credit card debt is the worst loan you can have. It's insidious and very expensive. We discuss it in more detail below.

There is an MBA loans program sponsored by the Graduate Management Admissions Council (which runs the GMAT). Its e-mail address is csn@northstar.org and its telephone number is 800 366-6227. It maintains a web site at http://www.gmat.org and has a complete portfolio of federal and private loan options for MBA students.

When you apply for loans or financial aid it is important to:

- meet all the deadlines—financial deadlines may be different from application deadlines;

- respond promptly if you are asked to send in more information or documents;
- make sure that the information is received by the Financial Aid Office; and
- be accurate, complete, honest, and neat when you fill out the financial aid application.

Also, keep a copy of every financial aid document you send and receive.

HOW IS YOUR CREDIT?

Anyone who hopes to secure a loan should be aware that financial aid programs take into account your credit rating before they agree to lend you money. If you have taken out a loan while you were an undergraduate, be sure that you are repaying it. If you have other debts, you may have to repay them before you start taking out new loans.

Be sure that you don't rack up unmanageable debts while in school. Students should especially be aware of credit cards. Poverty-stricken students often get alluring offers and, when you can hardly afford anything, some of these sound too good to refuse.

If you need more money, it is far better to get an additional student loan. Just the interest on a $5,000 credit card debt, not including the principal, will be about $75 per month, a lot of money for a graduate student.

SPECIFIC PROGRAMS

MEDICAL SCHOOL

Medical schools are expensive. Tuition and fees at medical schools can be more than $24,000 for one year. That amount doesn't cover the money you will need to pay for room, board, books and supplies, transportation, and personal expenses. And while you are in medical school, you do not have the same opportunity for teaching or research assistantships as students working on a Ph.D. do.

Medical students have to be in class many hours each week, and advanced students also do clinical work. Most medical schools do not want their students to have outside jobs. These programs demand so much time that students find it almost impossible to earn outside money while in school.

You probably will have to take out loans, but when you start your professional life you do not want to face paying back many hundreds of dollars every month. While the cost of a professional education has gone up and up, many new doctors find that their postgraduate incomes grow slowly, so slowly that they wonder whether they can pay back their debts, have a family life and even buy a house, or if they will be paying until they retire. To prevent that possibility, you will have to start early to search for funds. It may be difficult to find funding, but it is not impossible.

SOME SCHOLARSHIPS AVAILABLE

Start searching before you are notified that you have been accepted. The first step is to contact the medical school's financial aid officer. Ask him or her to help you make a financial plan for your years in medical school. There are always some scholarships or grants that are under the control of the medical school itself. Be sure to follow the procedure for applying for them. Other funds are awarded by the government or private foundations.

Some aid programs are available for students who will agree to practice for a certain number of years in a designated geographical area after they complete their medical education. These usually will pay for tuition and fees and sometimes a monthly stipend. As long as you practice where and for the length of time committed for, you will not have to repay the money.

These include the Armed Forces Scholarship Programs (Army, Navy, and Air Force) and the U.S. Public Health Service's National Health Service Corps and the Exceptional Financial Need Scholarship Program. The Indian Health Service also has a scholarship program that is primarily for Native Americans and is for students who commit themselves to primary care training and practice. Generally for these aid programs you have to agree to at least two years of service and will get a year of financial support for each year you serve.

There are a few scholarships for gifted students. These are great because you don't have to repay them. They do not add to the burden of debt you face, but many of them do not give out a huge amount of money. They are usually based on the student's academic merit, although for some, financial need is also considered. One is awarded by the American Association of University Women, but it is only for the final year of medical school. Books describing all of these sources, some specifically for medical students, are listed in the References.

Minority students should look at the Internet page of the Minority On-Line Information Service mentioned above. It has very complete information.

The Internet has a page on types of financial aid available for medical students. This lists books that discuss financial aid for medical students and also unusual loan sources for them. The address is http://www.finaid.org/finaid/focus/medical.html.

There are other sources of information on financial aid for medical school. The Association of American Medical Colleges, 11 Dupont Circle, NW, Washington, DC 20036, will help you learn about loans for medical students. The association also publishes a planning book, which is listed in the References.

But the best place to start is with your medical college's Financial Aid Office. When you apply to medical school, apply at the same time for financial aid. This will mean filling out an FAFSA form and any other documents the school asks for. Take it from there.

LAW SCHOOL

Law school, too, is expensive. Because the study of law is so demanding, law schools, like medical schools, generally do not want their students to take outside work, at least not in the first year.

Second- and third-year students can take advantage of opportunities to work and earn some money.

A good place to start is the free brochure *Financial Aid for Law School: A Preliminary Guide*, available from the Law School Admission Council. Their postal and Internet addresses are given in the Reference Addresses. The web site has a complete list of their publications, and you can order by e-mail.

One Internet site that gives a short but good summary of available financial aid is the Princeton Review page on financing law school. The address is http://www.review.com/faid/law_faid.html. Another Internet site at http://www.finaid.org/finaid/focus/law.html is the Law School Resources page, specifically for law school financial aid.

In addition, many law schools have pages on the Internet that give information about financial aid in their programs. For example, the Yale Law School's page says that it offers aid solely on the basis of need. As of this writing, the total costs there run about $32,000 a year, and 70 percent of the students get some financial aid. Even with this aid, the typical student owes $50,000 at graduation.

The University of Chicago, at the time you are admitted, will help you to make a three-year plan to cover your time in law school. The advisers consider academic achievement, work out a ratio of grants to loans that they think is appropriate, and encourage you to apply for financial aid right away.

Do not wait until you have used up your other support before applying for financial aid in any program.

FINANCIAL AID OFFICE

The best place to learn what funding is available is the law school's Financial Aid Office. Each office has a list of scholarships given by that school to students who show the greatest promise, or have the greatest need. The office also lists scholarships that are funded from the outside; many of these are earmarked for students with special qualifications, such as one provided by the Federation of Business and Professional Women's Clubs, or the grants provided by the

Council on Legal Education Opportunity for students from economically and educationally disadvantaged backgrounds.

To apply for loans, you will usually start by completing an FAFSA form. Follow the instructions given by the Financial Aid Office. Copy the application for your files and also keep copies of tax records and any supporting documents, in case you are asked to produce them.

While the Federal Direct Student (Stafford) Loans are funded by the government, the university approves your loan application and credits the loan directly to your account. There are subsidized loans for which you have to demonstrate need and unsubsidized loans that are not based on need. See the section on financial aid earlier in this chapter. Law school financial aid offices have lists of other loans for their students.

WORKING IN LAW SCHOOL

After their first year, some law students work as summer interns at law firms or with government agencies. In addition to the needed money, this work gives them experience in litigation, legal writing, or doing research. Other students may work as research assistants to professors, participating in the faculty members' scholarly work and publications. In addition to their salary, they may also get their tuition waived.

The Internet and books such as those listed in the References are invaluable. Think about it and plan ahead.

MONEY IS AVAILABLE

Remember, you can find financial aid. Start looking for it. Read the brochures carefully from the programs you are considering and see how much you can expect from each. Then contact the universities' financial aid offices, talk to the people there, and read their financial aid material. Surf the Internet and read the books and guides. Apply for external funds if you think you have a reasonable chance of succeeding. Above all, make your applications the best that you possibly can.

Every graduate student can find some money to help with the education he or she needs. It is there if you know how to look for it. Follow the advice in this chapter to get you off to a good start.

PART 2 APPLYING

CHAPTER 5

THE APPLICATION FORM

> *I* had a pretty good undergraduate record so I applied to four universities, two of them leaders in the field, the third a very good one and the fourth, in the next state, as insurance. One of the top ones turned me down; the place I had thought would be the fallback admitted me but said they would not give me any financial aid; the third one, which was ranked higher than the fallback, offered me a teaching assistantship; and the fourth, one of the top two, offered me a fellowship that covered all my expenses. Where do you think I went?
>
> **—JOHN**

THE NEXT STEP is filling out your applications. Applying to graduate school is much more involved than the word implies. The next few chapters will show you the best way to cope with this complicated procedure so that you will get into the program you want.

For each program you apply to, you will need to provide:

1. An application form;
2. Your statement, essay, or letter showing your intellectual development, and telling about your goals and why you are interested in that program (see Chapter 6);
3. Official transcripts of your undergraduate grades and any graduate courses and grades, sent in directly from every college you have attended (see Chapter 7);
4. At least two, usually three letters of recommendation sent directly to the department by the person, often a faculty member, who is writing the recommendation or by the college or institution that has kept the letters on file (see Chapter 7);

5. Graduate or professional examination scores sent in directly by the testing agency. Most graduate programs require an examination, such as the Graduate Record Examination (GRE) or for a professional program, a test in that field, such as the Graduate Management Admission Test (GMAT) or the Medical College Admission Test (MCAT). These scores are used to predict how successful you will be in that program (see Chapter 8);

6. Other materials, such as a portfolio of your work, depending on the program; and

7. Your application fee.

These requirements are discussed below.

STARTING THE PROCESS

Begin to get organized at least a year in advance. Collect information and send for admissions materials. Carefully reread the material each program sends you with its application form. Occasionally a school will have unusual requirements. It is important to send each school exactly what it asks for.

Most programs will not begin to look at your application until they receive all of the required materials.

For some programs it may take longer than a year to get together the best application possible. You will need more time if you apply for a national scholarship or if you want admission to a medical school. And if you are making a big change from your undergraduate study to a new field, say from history to medicine, you will probably have to take some undergraduate classes in order to get the prerequisite courses you need.

Apply to at least four or five programs, not just one or two.

As you will quickly realize, applying is not free. You have to send in a fee with your application to each program. You will also have to pay to take the GRE or other graduate admission tests, to send for transcripts, and to buy postage and photocopies. You may have the expenses of telephone calls and travel in addition. You may also want to spend money on test preparation books, or on taking a course. The process can be expensive; the minimum cost to send in several applications will be in the hundreds of dollars.

Check with the university's Graduate Admissions Office to see if financial need will enable you to apply without paying the fee when you send in your application.

Among the additional requirements for specific programs are these: If you are applying for an M.F.A. in writing, you may be asked to send a sample of your written work. For a master's in architecture, you will probably have to send in a portfolio, while a musician may have to pass an audition or send in a tape. Some liberal arts programs ask for a copy of a paper the applicant wrote as an undergraduate; a foreign language department may require a paper written in that language.

Max, who applied to an architecture program, had to send in a portfolio of his artwork. Max spent weeks getting together cartoons he had done, paintings, and photographs that showed furniture he had designed and models he had built. These elements are very important. It is worth spending time to make the portfolio as impressive as possible.

If the department requests a sample of work or a portfolio, follow the format specifications exactly even if they seem silly to you. Some places will simply reject applicants whose portfolios do not conform.

Send your application according to the instructions on it, usually to the university admissions office. That office makes a record of each graduate applicant, and then sends the application file to the department. If you do not include the fee or a fee waiver attached, the application may not be sent on.

FACULTY'S CHOICE

It is the department faculty who decide which applicants to admit. The university admissions office serves as a gateway: it has little to do with whether you are accepted, except for seeing that the university's rules are followed. The people you are really applying to are the members of your chosen department. You are preparing to work in a specific field, and the experts are the ones who will decide whether they want you.

If your goal is a Ph.D. in history, your application will be reviewed by professors in the history department. They will be able to admit only a certain number, and because of a limited budget can offer financial aid to even fewer. You need to prove to them that you deserve admission and support.

Admission is actually granted by the institution, not the department or the program. If your admission is recommended by the department it is almost certain that you will be admitted by the university, but not quite. The university may have strict rules; a grade point average above a minimum is a common requirement. If you are a brilliant physics student with a low average because of your humanities course grades, you may still get into graduate school, but it's harder. You will have to find a program that wants you enough to petition the admissions office for a waiver of the rule in your case. The faculty won't take the trouble to do this unless you are exceptional. They may wonder whether, if you didn't care enough to get decent grades, you can succeed as a graduate student. They will be particularly wary about awarding financial aid to such an applicant.

THE APPLICATION FORM

Your application form is the first piece of information the faculty members know about you. How can yours make a good impression?

You should be sure that your application:

1. contains all the information asked for;
2. is correct, neat, and readable; and
3. arrives in time.

Before beginning to work on the form, make a photocopy and work on that, or type your answers separately, using a computer. Read all the questions carefully and answer each one on the copy.

It will hurt your chances if the application is not neat or words are not spelled correctly. Professors may have to read dozens of applications. They are not going to spend time trying to figure out what you mean. If the form is messy, if words are misspelled, if what you write is ungrammatical, if tenses don't agree, the application makes a bad impression and may be put, without careful reading, in the reject pile.

Some people feel that a person who makes mistakes in English usage, if he or she is not foreign-born, does not belong in graduate school. This is particularly true in liberal arts programs. When you review the application you can use a spellchecker, but to be sure that every word is the one you want, you will have to proofread it yourself. Get someone else to read it, too.

You are competing with people who are sending in neat, correct, and legible applications. Before you mail out your application, read it over with a critical eye and make corrections. This point cannot be emphasized too strongly. Remember, this is going to be read by professionals in your chosen area.

When each application is as good as you can make it, before you mail it, make a photocopy to keep handy in case your original gets lost after you send it in.

Sometimes the application form is also the form on which you request financial aid. Other times the request for financial aid is separate. Be aware, pay attention, ask questions. You want to make sure that you apply for everything for which you want to be considered.

At many schools, the applicants who request financial aid are considered separately, and the committee decides earlier about them than about those who don't ask for financial aid. This is why the deadlines for the financial aid form and the application may be different.

The committee members who read your application will pay more attention if you are being considered for aid. You are asking for a financial commitment from them, and they take very seriously the job of awarding aid packages. They have limited funds, a definite number of teaching assistantships and fellowships available for entering graduate students, and they want to use them to get the best possible entering class for their program.

A MYSTERY

How the departments choose which students to admit and which will get financial aid is a mystery, known only to the faculty who make the decisions. What a committee decides may be different from one year to the next, depending on the department's budget, as well as the qualifications of the other applicants. Since the members on the committee change from time to time, a student rejected one year might have been accepted by the same department in a different year. Even so, it's generally not a good idea to apply to a program that previously turned you down. The reviewers will know that you were rejected, and that won't help. It's usually better to apply someplace new.

Two faculty committees can look at the same application and come to different conclusions. The fate of an application can partly depend on which faculty members read your application, what their interests are and what is happening in the department at the time. That is why applying to several places is wise.

THE INSIDE STORY: HOW THE FACULTY DECIDES WHICH STUDENTS TO ADMIT
It will help you to know how graduate students are chosen, and why some are admitted, others rejected. Applications for the following academic year start to come in during the fall semester. The faculty member who serves as the department's primary admissions officer, usually the Graduate Adviser, reads each one as it arrives. People whose grades are far below the department's standard or who do not have the prerequisite course work may be rejected immediately. All complete applications that are above a minimum standard are kept for further examination. If an application is incomplete, the department will probably send a card telling the applicant what is

missing. If the deadline has passed, and the department has plenty of applications, late or incomplete applications will go into the reject pile. Occasionally, with a superior applicant, if part of the application is missing, the department will make an effort, by phone or e-mail, to contact the applicant and get the missing pieces. This will happen only if some faculty member wants to see the full application for this particular applicant.

Large departments may receive several hundred applications, which are parceled out in groups to different committees. Most faculty members on these committees have a pretty clear idea of the levels of ability of graduate students already in the department, and will judge the applicants by these standards. In a small department with fewer applicants, all the applications may be read by one committee, or by almost every faculty member.

The men and women on the committee begin to meet in the winter. They read each application carefully. Some members pay particular attention to the essay, others do not; but you have to convince them all. They look at the grade point average, GRE or other test scores, and the transcripts of grades. They note the number and level of courses the student has taken in the field, and grades in the major, particularly for the last 60 hours of classes, as it is during the junior and senior years that the student shows his or her ability in the major field. They also want applicants who have at least satisfied the requirements for an undergraduate major in their own department.

They know that different colleges have different standards for undergraduate work. When reviewers look at a student's grades, they try to take into account how demanding the college is and how easy or difficult it is for a student at that school to get good grades.

They examine samples of the student's academic or creative work, such as a portfolio sent in by a potential architect or a tape from someone who wants an advanced degree in music composition. For some degrees, such as an M.B.A., work experience is important, and the committee members see how it is related to the proposed graduate program.

They read the letters of recommendation very carefully, noting the enthusiasm and whom they are from. Committee members pay more attention to recommendations sent by people they have heard of or know personally, so ask around among your undergraduate faculty to see if any connections exist between them and professors at the schools where you are are thinking of applying.

Each committee member then ranks the students in order, from the top one who has excellent grades, test scores, and recommendations, and who he or she feels would do superior work, all the way down to those whose scores are so low that they seem to have no chance of succeeding at that university. One professor's first choice may be far down on another's list. Then meetings will be held at which each explains his or her reasons; they argue until a final ranking is made.

Sometimes these are political decisions, in which faculty favor applicants who show interest in their own particular area of research. This series of meetings can become a battleground where the future direction of the department is influenced.

In a small committee, one professor's opinion can be very important, especially if it is very high or low. If one committee member thinks you are great, that can do wonders for you. On the other hand, if one member thinks you are a bad prospect and argues against you, you probably won't be admitted and certainly won't be offered financial aid. Committees, not only faculty committees, tend to behave a little bit like animal herds; a strong opinion can push the whole committee one way or the other. A member might think, "Well, I'm not so impressed with this applicant, but Professor Jones is. Let's take a chance and see what this student can do." This is particularly true if Jones has a reason for his opinion, such as knowing that a good recommendation was written by a person with very high standards.

When they have finished discussing the applicants, the committee as a whole puts them in order for the final list. Many committees decide at that time which are the top students who will get fellowships and teaching assistantships.

RESEARCH MONEY FOR SCIENCE STUDENTS

In some well-funded departments, mainly in science and engineering, admissions are determined differently. In those departments, students are admitted as research assistants rather than as teaching assistants. Their applications are circulated among faculty members who have research money; they choose which students they want to provide funds for. It helps if the student has already chosen a field and asked to study with a particular professor. If a student is exceptionally qualified, several faculty members may want him or her. The professor with the most prestige may be the one who wins that student.

HOW THE DEPARTMENT MANAGES ITS OFFERS

Each department has a budget that limits what the admissions committee can do. The faculty members have to estimate how many people they can offer financial aid to for the next year. Usually they make the offers in March or early April—the standard deadline for acceptances is April 15—and at that time they do not know how many of their current graduate students will remain and how many places will be available to take in new ones. Sometimes a student plans to return the following fall but gets a job somewhere, changes plans, and simply fails to show up when the semester starts. Also, it may not be known until after March what fellowship and assistantship funds will definitely be available. After they know, or have estimated, how much money they have, the committee decides how many new students they can fund.

This is a difficult situation for an academic program. The faculty don't know how many of their current TAs will definitely return in the fall. They don't know what percentage of offers they make will be accepted. They may not even know for sure whether they will have funds for the number of TAs the department needs for next year. The situation is so fluid that good students may end up without an offer, or poor students may get one. So, if you don't initially get an award but all of your feedback was good, don't give up on the prospect of grad school. You can try again next year or, if you were denied at some school because of a temporary financial crisis there and can manage the gamble, accept an offer with no aid and hope for financial aid later.

A FIRM COMMITMENT

All faculty members want the best graduate students to come to their department, so they give a lot of thought to choosing which ones they will offer financial aid. These offers are firm commitments by the university.

Because no one is certain which of the students who are accepted will come to this university and which will go somewhere else, many departments operate like an airline, admitting more than they have spaces for, and hope that they have guessed right. After all, students apply to several universities and often choose the one that gives them the best financial aid.

But, unlike with an airline, students who are accepted cannot be bumped. If you are admitted, the school will honor the offer even if it is badly overcommitted. And if you get a letter offering you financial aid, you will receive the money if you accept.

In 1996, Cornell University had thirty more acceptances for its M.D. program than it had spaces for. They offered a year of free tuition, at $24,000, to any student who would delay starting for a year. But those who did not delay had to be enrolled.

Other departments make only as many offers as they have places available. If a student declines, an offer is immediately made to the next student on the list. Of course, by that time the student may have committed to some other university. Students are pleased and happy to get an offer; when the offer is late, they draw the conclusion that they are not in the top group of applicants, and they are right. Departments that operate this way may fail to get enough students, or the students may be of lower quality, but the departments do not extend themselves beyond their budgets.

DECISION-MAKING IS NOT PERFECT

The process of deciding which students to admit is very idiosyncratic. Even the most rigorous committees do not make perfect decisions. Different faculty committees can look at the same application and come to different conclusions.

The faculty members of departments are in a continual state of change. Aside from retirements and newly hired faculty, professors may take sabbatical leaves and leaves of absence to work at other universities. The head of an academic department often serves for only a few years, and when he or she steps down the new person may exercise power differently and make many changes. New department heads and other administrators usually have little training for the job and may not be aware of all the rules and procedures. This lack of continuity can lead to variations in the process for admitting students from one year to the next.

The foregoing does not describe the practices of every department. However, it's an unavoidable fact that departmental administrators and committees change, and a well-thought-out process may be replaced by one that is quite strange. If you are rejected—or accepted, for that matter—don't assume that the process was completely rational.

So what does this mean to you, and how should you proceed?

IT TAKES TIME

As we keep saying, allow yourself plenty of time. Getting everything together is going to take longer than you think.

Ten years after she graduated, Karen realized that she did not want to spend the rest of her life in advertising. There must be more to life than photographing tacos and bowls of corn flakes, she thought, when there was this big world outside, full of plants and people and countryside that needed to be protected. What she really wanted to do was to work in landscape architecture. But her undergraduate major was English, a far different field, and what was worse, her grades were not very good.

Her application had to show that now she was mature enough to work hard as a student, and had the qualifications to do good work as a landscape architect, and it had to explain why she was making this career change. She worked hard on it. She knew her academic record would not earn her any financial aid before she enrolled, particularly since she was changing her field, so she planned to borrow some money and hoped she would get an assistantship later.

She visited the University of California at Berkeley to talk to a professor in landscape architecture. When the professor heard that Karen was an English major and had been working in advertising, the professor said bluntly that she would not be accepted because she did not have the right qualifications.

At that point Karen wondered if she should just give up. But she did not. Instead she worked hard on her essay. And then she spent weeks getting together her drawings and paintings, as well as the best of the photographs she had taken. She spent a great deal of time placing them in the portfolio she was required to submit.

Karen applied to eight schools. She was accepted by three programs, put on the waiting list by one, told by another that it would consider her if she first enrolled as an undergraduate, and turned down by the others. UC-Berkeley was her first choice, and that is where she went.

What Karen did shows how important it is to spend time making your application really good. After she started class, another professor told her that her portfolio was the reason the committee had accepted her, and that he had been intrigued by the artistry shown in the photographs.

John, who was Phi Beta Kappa at an Ivy League school and had graduated with honors in physics, had a different problem. He wanted to change his field, and needed to support himself while he was working on a Ph.D. in mathematics. He had to show that he was good enough in mathematics for the department to give him an assistantship, which would enable him to live and to compete with students who had been in mathematics from the start.

While he was working full time, he went as a non-degree student to a good university nearby, where he took two advanced math courses. He did well, and got good recommendations from those professors.

John was rejected by one school, and admitted by another but with no financial aid. A third offered him a teaching assistantship, and the fourth, his first choice, the State University of New York at Stony Brook, awarded him a fellowship, which he accepted. At least two of the other three schools were not ranked as highly as Stony Brook was in mathematics.

The non-degree status is reserved for students who are not working toward a degree, who just want to take a course or two. It could be the spouse of a faculty member or someone in the community who needs a course in accounting or economics. The department makes no commitment to such students beyond giving them instruction in the classes they take, and these students can be denied admission to any course which is full or, if for any reason, the instructor does not want them in the class. However, credits earned as a non-degree student can count toward a degree if the student's status is changed. It is much easier to be admitted as a non-degree student, and this can be a route to later admission as a degree student.

Getting admitted to any program is never a sure bet. John's experience is revealing, because it shows just how random the admissions process is. Faculty committees in different schools, with different priorities, will view the same applicant, with similar essays and the same recommendations, transcripts, and test scores, in completely different ways. That is why it is essential that you should apply to several programs, not just one or two. This is particularly important for the most sought-after degrees, such as the M.B.A. Students who want to be sure to be admitted often apply to as many as ten or fifteen programs.

PROFESSIONAL SCHOOL APPLICATIONS

If you are applying to law, medical, dental, osteopathy, podiatry, or veterinary medical school, you may have to use a national application or data assembly program. These services gather information from applicants, put it into a standardized form, and send it on to the professional schools, where it is added to materials that the applicant has provided, such as letters of recommendation and the application itself. Any adviser in your field will be able to tell you whether there is a national application service.

LAW SCHOOL DATA ASSEMBLY SERVICE (LSDAS)

If you are interested in law school, your first step is to get the *LSAT & LSDAS Registration and Information Book,* which is issued by the Law School Admission Council (LSAC), also known as Law Services. The council's address is given in the Reference Addresses section at the end of this book. Most law schools will have copies of this free book.

The book contains all the information you need to register for the LSAT and to "subscribe," as the book puts it, to the LSDAS. It contains the forms you must fill out to do both of these things.

Here is what you have to do, and what Law Services does. In essence, you provide the LSAC with information, and the council sends it on, in the form of standardized reports, to the law schools where you are applying.

You must take, or have taken, the LSAT. You must also have a current LSDAS subscription; a subscription is good for a year, and costs about $100. When you subscribe, you give them fairly complete personal information by filling out machine-readable forms that are provided. You also have to list information on every college, graduate, or professional school you ever attended, including its name, an identifying code number, when you were there, your major, and your degree or date of expected degree. Separately, you have to request an official transcript from the registrar's office of each of these institutions to be sent to Law Services (forms are provided, and you will have to include a fee). You do not tell Law Services which law schools you are applying to. You send a fee to cover the number of reports that you will want sent out (one report is included with your subscription fee), and the law schools request reports directly from Law Services. Your actual applications with essays, and the letters of recommendation, are your responsibility; Law Services is not involved in this part of the process.

THE LAW SERVICES REPORT

After you subscribe, sending in the information Law Service requests, it will send you a subscription confirmation. When all of your transcripts have been received and the LSDAS summary has been completed, you will get a Master Law School Report. You should check this report for accuracy. Law Services will send a copy of the report to the law schools that request it, up to the number you have paid for. It will also send you a report every month if any activity in your file has occurred, beginning about a month after your Law Services file has been established. This includes such information as the names of law schools that have asked for your report that month, transcripts that have been received, transcripts you requested that have not yet been received, and whether or not Law Services has your annual renewal.

The report sent to the law schools contains your biographical information, a detailed summary of all your college grades and credits with recalculated grade point averages, photocopies of all your transcripts, all reportable LSAT results since June 1, 1992, photocopies of up to three of your most recent LSAT writing samples, a notation indicating whether you have ever been the subject of a misconduct or irregularity determination, and, if requested by the law school, an admission index.

An admission index is a combination of an applicant's LSAT score and grade point average into a single number. Law schools with many more applicants than they can possibly admit may use such an index as a cutoff, and reject any applicant whose index is below a chosen level. In order for such an index to be useful, all grade point averages must be calculated in the same way. Law Services does recalculate all GPAs, so the reported GPA may not agree with one calculated by the college. For example, physical education courses with an assigned grade and credit are included in the calculation, but courses that are designated as remedial are not.

The LSDAS is not free, but it does liberate you from some worries. You are kept informed of whether your transcripts have arrived, and when the reports are sent to your law schools. You know that your personal information document is treated like all the others, and you have a chance to check it over before it is sent out. You know that your GPA will be recalculated so that a level comparison can be made between you and the other applicants.

AMERICAN MEDICAL COLLEGES APPLICATION SERVICE

AMCAS is run by the Association of American Medical Colleges, and is similar to the LSDAS. The AMCAS address is given in the Reference Addresses section at the end of this book. You submit your complete application with essay and transcripts, but without letters of recommendation, to AMCAS, and the service sends it on to the medical schools. This means that each of the AMCAS medical schools receives the same materials; you cannot tailor your application to the school. For example, the service requires that the essay you submit be on just one page. If a school wants anything nonstandard in its application forms, that school cannot use AMCAS. In fact, about ten percent of U.S. medical schools, including Harvard and Yale, do not use AMCAS. For such schools you will have to send the application directly to the school, in accordance with their instructions.

You can submit your application electronically (if you have a computer that uses Windows) by using the AMCAS-E service. You can download the necessary software from the AMCAS web site, use it, and submit your application on a diskette.

However you submit it, AMCAS will check to see that your application is complete, and will verify that your transcripts are correct by checking with the schools that provided them. When AMCAS sends the application materials to the medical schools you specify, your last two MCAT scores are included. The medical schools then notify the applicants about required letters of recommendation and fees. The MCAT announcement booklet lists the medical schools that use AMCAS and also the medical schools that do not.

WHAT YOU NEED

Get your application in on time. To sum up, when you apply you need the following:

1. An application form—make it neat, be sure it's complete;
2. Your statement, essay, or letter telling about yourself and your goals; this is usually part of the application;

3. Official transcripts of all of your undergraduate and graduate course grades sent in to the programs directly by the colleges with the institution's official seal (photocopies made by you probably will not be acceptable);

4. Letters of recommendation sent directly to the department by the person who is writing the recommendation, or by an institution that has kept the letters on file;

5. Graduate or professional examination scores sent in directly by the testing agency;

6. Other materials, such as an art portfolio or a tape, depending on what the program asks for; and

7. Your application fee.

Your application, with its supporting material, is probably the most important single piece of work in your life so far. A fellowship or teaching assistantship, with a tuition waiver, can easily be worth $50,000 to a master's degree student, and well over $100,000 to a doctoral student. Spend time to make your application the best it can be.

6

THE ESSAY

> *Writing the essay was difficult. My grades were nothing to brag about, and I knew the essay had to make up for them. It took me days of writing and rewriting, but finally I finished one. My adviser later told me the essay was the reason they admitted me.*
>
> **—FRANCES**

THE ESSAY QUESTION is the most important part of your application, says Graduate College Dean Gaye Wong of the University of Illinois at Urbana-Champaign. Your application reveals your grades, your test performance, and what other people think of you. The essay is the place where you show what *you* can do.

This may be called Objectives of Graduate Study, or Statement of Purpose or something like Personal Background. Whatever its name, it is the place where you become something more than a statistic on a page. It is where the professors who read your application find out what kind of person you are. It is in the essay that you have the best chance of pulling away from the pack.

The essay is like a personal interview, one that you have the time and opportunity to shape to show yourself off at your best.

A good essay not only can determine whether you get admitted (particularly if your grades and other materials are only average), but may also make a difference in whether you get an assistantship or no money at all. A bad essay may sink you.

You have to convince the committee members that you are a student the department really wants. How do you do this?

DON'T START WRITING YET

Start thinking early and allow yourself plenty of time. Do not begin by writing the essay itself. Instead, take a pad of paper and jot down a summary of your life. List your family, your education, your jobs. What are your strengths, your weaknesses, your goals? What makes you unique? What have you done that makes you proud? What are your educational achievements, and how do you want to continue your intellectual development? How have you responded to past disappointments or failures? Write it all down, even items you would not consider including in the final essay. While this may seem like a lot of work, it is background that you can draw on for all the essays you write.

In Chapter 1 you were encouraged to think about your reasons for going to graduate school. Use what you wrote then as a source. Once you start thinking about your life, more will come to mind. What are the good things you have done, and the not so good? Be sure to put down any honors or prizes you have received. Also list any gaps you might have to explain away, such as the two years you spent flipping hamburgers.

WHAT THE FACULTY LOOKS FOR

The committee members want to find out whether you are prepared for graduate study, able to do it well, and are focused. They want to know that you are committed to this subject, how you got interested in it, and what you hope to get out of graduate school. They are more interested in your intellectual than in your personal development.

They want to know what you plan to do after you receive your degree and what you have in mind for the future. You may not be all that sure yourself, but tell them as much as you can, with as much conviction as you can muster. They look for evidence that you are committed enough to make graduate education worthwhile, and that you will stick with it.

Remember whom you are writing for. Your readers are educated faculty members, and all of them are interested in their subject. Their professional lives are committed to work in the field, to teaching, research, and public service.

The faculty want students to work with as colleagues. If you do not have a strong interest in the field, you should probably not go to graduate school. You must make it clear that you do have this interest, that you are willing and able to invest the time and talent necessary to become a professional.

They also want to know if you can write clearly and convey your ideas well. In almost all professions, it is important to be able to communicate. Muddy or confused statements give a bad impression, and one bad impression can cause you to be turned down. If you don't hold the reader's attention, you may end up in the reject pile.

Different fields attract different kinds of people, and you need to adjust your writing style accordingly. If you are applying in science or engineering, concentrate more on the facts of your life than on your hopes, dreams, and aspirations. It's all right to say that you have always had a deep interest in chemistry, and to back it up with some facts. It probably won't help to say that the romance of chemistry strikes sparks in your soul. Tailor your letter, and the style of your writing, to your audience.

Before you begin to write, read the instructions again for each program you are applying to. Some may ask for an essay of no more than 300 words, others want at least 500 words; many do not mention length at all. Remember that each committee member will be reading dozens, even hundreds, of applications. If an essay is only half of a double-spaced page, it's not really an essay. If it runs over three pages, it's a little daunting to the reader; there's a temptation to skim. If no precise length is specified, one to two typed pages is a good length.

If the instructions specify topics you are supposed to cover, follow the directions. Some application forms are far less detailed than others and just say something like "State your reasons for undertaking graduate work and your specific interest with respect to the program for which you are applying. You may include career objectives, research interests and experience." But you should write more than this. This is your opportunity to show the people who read it why you are a student they want.

One English professor says that he looks for three things in application essays. They are intellectual development, knowledge of the field, and the ability to write well and clearly.

You would like the professor who reads it to think, "Hey, this is a pretty good essay—writes well—knows what she wants from our program—has a couple of original ideas—let's get her here."

SOME ESSAY QUESTIONS

Different schools ask different questions. For example, among other questions, the J. L. Kellogg Graduate School of Management at Northwestern University recently asked students to describe in one or two double-spaced pages how their backgrounds, experiences, and values would enhance the diversity of the student body. Students were also asked to answer other questions in one or two paragraphs. One was about the applicant's most valued accomplishment; another asked about the greatest issue the applicant continues to struggle with.

On its application form, Carnegie Mellon University's top-ranked computer science department instructs its applicants for the Ph.D. program to type a one- or two-page concise statement addressing these points:

1. State your objective in pursuing a Ph.D. in computer science and why you chose to apply to Carnegie Mellon.
2. Describe your background in computer science and other fields relevant to your objective. List here any relevant industrial or commercial experience.
3. Include any additional information you wish to supply to the admissions committee.

Students applying for a liberal arts program at the University of California at Irvine were asked to:

"State your general reasons for undertaking graduate work and your specific interest with respect to the program in which you are applying. The admissions committee must determine whether or not your objective can be satisfied within that program. You may wish to include career objectives, research interests and experience and your intended area of specialization. Please give a brief occupational resumé if any significant period has elapsed since you were last enrolled in an academic institution. Type or print clearly."

At the University of Illinois at Urbana-Champaign, a prospective student in a liberal arts program is told:

"Please attach a statement of not more than 300 words concerning your previous academic work in your proposed or allied field of study, including course work, other educational experiences, teaching or other relevant employment, publications, and your plans for graduate study and a professional career."

START WITH A DRAFT

Now, get started. This is a first draft, not the essay you are sending out, so you can be honest. Tell about yourself and why you are applying to this program. In the first draft you can boast, you can write down things that make you squirm with embarrassment. Put in sentences you will condense in subsequent drafts or omit altogether. The important thing is to get down enough material so you can shape it into an essay that is a winner. Do not just repeat information you have already given on the application form or on your transcript of grades.

WHAT TO INCLUDE

The committee is interested in your plans for the future. Tell them what they are. What do you want to do after you get your degree? Do you want to do research in physics at a university, design computer software, open a restaurant? Do you want to teach history in a community college, be a lawyer who specializes in international contracts, or become a nurse-midwife?

Faculty members want students who are intellectually involved in their fields. Write about what you have done, or thought, besides taking the required courses for your major. Include relevant facts about yourself, particularly any honors.

In part of her essay an applicant in education wrote:

> *For the past three summers I have assisted Professor Greta Stone of the Education College in teaching a program designed to help disadvantaged inner-city girls become proficient in reading. This program has not only improved their test scores but has increased their self-esteem and desire to remain in school. To watch some of these young women who have had so little encouragement become excited about reading and confident about themselves has given me as much pleasure as the award I received, the Jane Addams Fellowship for superior work.*

Don't go on at length about your feelings and self-development. Graduate programs are not there to help people with their personal development; they are there for study and research, and to create professionals in the field. Professors want to admit students who can do the difficult work; they do not care much about helping a graduate student in self-realization.

FACING PROBLEMS

This is the time to face some potential difficulties. If your transcript shows you had a bad semester or two, explain how you dealt with that. Were your grades as an undergraduate not so good because you had to work many hours a week to support yourself? Or because you were immature and now have grown up and realize how important continuing your education is?

Here is what one student wrote:

> *Unlike the classical image of a prospective graduate student, I do not have a perfect grade point average. My earlier disappointing grades are from the past. As evidenced by my work of the last year, I have left these anomalies where they belong: behind me. At present I am an A student and expect to remain one. Moreover, I am an A student in*

advanced courses, which are more difficult than run-of-the-mill courses and give me an opportunity to demonstrate talent and creativity.

But you must explain any difficulty in a way that does not hurt your chances; do not write something like this, from a man whose GRE scores were not good:

I would like to address the reason for my less than excellent GRE scores. I feel that I do not test well on standardized testing, and those scores do not fully reflect my ability to be successful in graduate study. I hope you will consider my other qualifications.

This did not help. In physics, the field he was applying to enter, every graduate student has to take many tests, and a student who does not test well is not likely to do well. This student would have helped himself if he had emphasized that although his GRE scores were not so great his grades were good, and that grades are a better reflection of ability than the test scores, because grades show the result of sustained work. If he had a special reason, such as that he was dyslexic or that he came from a non-English speaking family, he should have pointed that out.

OTHER PROBLEMS

If there is a time gap in your resumé, a committee will also want to know what you were doing then. If you spent years in a blue collar job, tell them about it. But also tell them how that relates to your proposed field of study. You can show that even during that time, you were amassing experiences that will be worthwhile in the new field. Maybe while you had a McJob you analyzed the different customers, some of whom seemed badly in need of help, and decided to become a social worker, or you watched the cash flow and got interested in accounting.

Returning students can turn their interim activities into strengths. While you were juggling time and car pool arrangements, did you realize that what you were doing was similar to managing a small business, or did you decide you enjoyed children and would like to teach kindergarten? Think about it. A number of unusual things that you may have done could have some relationship to the field. One thing in your favor is that older returning students on the whole do very well when they go back to school. The faculty members know this.

And, if you are working, do you have a convincing reason for giving up your current career? Tell them why you plan to make this big change. One student wrote:

> *Even though I was on the Dean's List for two semesters and had a fellowship for my freshman and sophomore years, after I graduated from Cornell with a B.A. in psychology I could find no suitable job. I worked for a while as a computer operator. I like computers, but in my job there was not enough challenge.*
>
> *I have always enjoyed making things, so I headed out to Hollywood where I worked on and off as a carpenter on movie sets, using some computer modeling but not much. After several years during which I witnessed a number of workers getting hurt on the job, I realized that there was a need for better and safer tools. I was taking a night school course in computer design when I saw what could be done with computers and knew then that I wanted to learn all that I could about computer-aided design. I am applying for admission to Illinois's industrial design program because of your strong program in computer graphics and its application to design.*

It also helps if you can give evidence of mental activity. Maybe you read many books in the field, or became an expert on silent films, or took a night school course as this student did.

PARTS OF ESSAYS THAT HELPED
Here is the start of one letter:

> *As far back as I can remember, I have wanted to be a mathematician. My mother said that by fourth grade, when asked what I wanted to be when I grew up, I always answered, "A college math professor." And after nearly three years of college, over a dozen mathematics courses*

(including several graduate courses) and approximately 1,000 hours of tutoring, I am more sure than ever that this is my destined profession. I don't know yet what I will specialize in, but I am now working hard on a course in measure theory, and am thinking about analysis.

I have been tutoring for over five years, waiting for the chance to teach an entire math class instead of just one student at a time. With all the practice I've had tutoring, I am one of the most highly recommended tutors on campus, being recommended by several of Purdue's science counselors.

Teaching members of Purdue's football team, I am also the highest paid tutor who is still an undergraduate.

This essay showed that the student was committed to mathematics and had been for many years, and that he had done work in the field he was choosing. Because he had already tutored and been recognized for the excellence of his teaching, he would be a good prospect. He was admitted with an assistantship.

Another applicant who was in a different area but had the same deep interest in the field she was choosing wrote:

I want to go to medical school to become a pediatrician and to cure sick children. There is such a great need for doctors to work with the poor and helpless, and I feel that this is my calling. For as long as I can remember it has been my goal. In high school when I took biology, then chemistry and physics, I worked hard and did well. I knew I needed to learn these subjects in order to go on to premed and medical school and I enjoyed getting a solid foundation in science.

For several years I've been a hospital volunteer, and last summer I had a job in a clinic laboratory.

This student was also admitted to medical school. The writing of both of these students was plain and clear. This type of essay probably wouldn't have helped them in a program such as a Master of Fine Arts in creative writing, where the applicant's essay should show originality and style.

SHOW THAT YOU WANT THIS SPECIFIC PROGRAM

What is in the school, and the program, in particular, that appeals to you? It's a good idea to show you are familiar with it and to say why you are applying there. It shows those who read your application that you are serious and are the kind of student who has taken the trouble to learn about their program.

The faculty are the ones who have shaped the program, and they naturally feel that theirs is a good one. A student who shows that he or she has looked at graduate schools and then chooses theirs has an advantage over an applicant who doesn't seem to know the difference between one program and the next.

Avoid phrases such as "your department has a very strong reputation" without mentioning the name of the university. It reads too much like a computer-printed letter that tells you, and 50,000 other people, that "because of your strong interest in the environment we are offering you . . ." It's still better if you mention something in the particular program. For example:

> Cornell's English department with its world renowned faculty and extensive library, as well as its excellent literary magazine Epoch, make your graduate program my first choice. I have just begun to have some of my writing published. I want to continue and to study with your Kathryn Newcastle Curley, an original and gifted writer. If given the opportunity to improve my own skills, I believe I have the ability to succeed at it.

Another student finished his essay with this paragraph. It's not quite as convincing, because it is less specific, but it's much better than a generic statement of praise for the department:

> For as long as I can remember I have been interested in the biological sciences. I would like to spend my life doing research in the field. The best way to prepare for this is to learn all I can from the best physiologists who are doing exciting work in a stimulating environment. I believe that UIUC's rigorous and demanding program will help me to develop my abilities to the greatest possible extent. My re-

search interests are in neurophysiology and cellular physiology, and it is no secret that UIUC offers a superlative program in these disciplines.

Now that you have decided on a new direction for your life, the faculty who have already chosen that field will agree that you have made a wise decision.

WRITING IT

The essay is one of the most important pieces of writing you will ever do. Take your time with it. You have a lot of information to get into the statement, and you will want to write it over until it is as clear and concise as you can make it. When you finish a draft, read it over. Then ask yourself, How can I make it more effective? Does it show clearly that I am committed to work hard, that I have the ability to earn a degree, and that I have good preparation?

When you have written the best statement you can and it says what you want it to say, read the essay out loud to yourself. Sometimes your ear hears mistakes that your eye doesn't see. Is your grammar correct, and have you avoided slang, clichés, and pompous language?

Then get someone else to read and critique it. Is there something you should not have put in? Or something that you forgot? Does it sound too boastful? If so, can you give concrete examples to back up your claims? Or perhaps you tear yourself down too much—a problem many women have. Be honest about your achievements; this is no time for false modesty.

When the essay is as good as you can make it, have it laser printed. Then make a copy of the entire application form, including the essay. Keep it in a safe place. After you've worked so hard to perfect this, you can probably use some, though not all of the essay for other graduate schools.

KIM'S MISTAKE

Whatever you do, don't do what Kim did. He applied to a Big Ten physics department and wrote in his letter of intent that he had wanted to be a physicist ever since he'd been a child, and explained what he liked about physics and what research he'd done as an undergraduate and what he wanted to do. Unfortunately for him, the physics department rejected him. Instead of writing a new application, he telephoned and asked for his application materials to be sent to the mathematics department.

The math professors on the admissions committee read that Kim had always wanted to be a physicist. Quite understandably, they decided there was no point in letting him in to study math, since it was not what he was interested in. So they, too, turned him down.

TWO WHOSE ESSAYS WRECKED THEIR CHANCES

Tell enough on your essay. Here is what one student wrote:

> *Statement in support of application:*
> *I have an M.S. from the University in Computer Science. I am considering work towards a Ph.D. in the fall of '95. Pursuant to this I would like to pick up some additional courses. Thus, the application for admission.*

This was his complete essay. He was not admitted.

Another candidate had not read the instructions. Instead of an essay she merely listed the courses she had taken, wrote two sentences about one of the courses, and then said:

> *I plan to earn a master's and possibly a doctorate. I would like to teach on a college level. I know I do not possess a strong background in teaching. Yet I know I can gain the experience and necessary skills to excel in graduate school.*

This did not tell the committee anything about her. She, too, was rejected.

ESSAYS THAT WORKED

Following are several essays that got their writers admitted to the programs they applied to. Most are for programs in the humanities, but one is from a law school applicant, one from a student in urban planning and one from a student in applied psychology.

In scientific and technological fields, essays are not as important as grade point averages, graduate examinations, and recommendations. The essays below are for programs in which the admissions committees read them very seriously, thought them over, compared them to others, discussed them and judged them to be winners.

Because committee decisions are made privately, it is not possible to say which parts of these essays convinced the faculty to admit these applicants, but as you look at the essays you can see that the applicants described their goals, their past experience, and why they wanted to go into their chosen field. Each one conveyed the idea that the writer was serious and committed and gave some indication of the writer's personality and interests. They concentrate on intellectual rather than personal development.

These are actual essays. In order to protect the students' privacy, names of colleges and faculty as well as other identifying details have been changed, as they have been in the essays above.

But, as was stressed earlier, when *you* write *your* essay, be sure to be specific. Name the university and the program to which you are applying and the faculty with whom you want to work, as well as the schools you have attended and the faculty with whom you have previously studied.

ENGLISH

Over the past five years while I have been completing my undergraduate education and working on my master's degree, I have also been figuring out where I fit into the academic world of literature, theory and criticism. My undergraduate studies at Wesley College gave me a broad grounding in the history of literature; now, in my graduate work at Washington University, I am exploring the interdisciplinary connections surrounding literature—in particular, literary theory. At this point, I am eager to continue my studies, and I feel that Cornell University would be the right place to do so.

My specific areas of interest have come into focus this year at Washington University where I am exploring the interdisciplinary contexts of literature by taking classes in religious studies as well as in social thought. Working with my mentor, Gerald Hoff, has stimulated my interest in questions of textuality and contextuality. Does the text exist prior to interpretation? What are the roles of belief and ideology in appreciation and interpretation? What are the uses of religious rhetoric in critical discourse?

I am interested in applying these broader questions to the historical literary context which most fascinates me—the nineteenth-century novel. My interest in this subject was sparked by a graduate class on "Realism in the Novel," taught by the novelist John Black. I could see myself doing work on the role of the author in the novel and an exploration of how the multiplicity of voices which characterizes novelistic discourse both includes and excludes the voice of the author. Pursuing this in a large-scale project such as a dissertation would mean engaging the current debate over whether the author has agency and individual subjectivity or is merely a conduit for intersubjective codes.

A related question which presented itself to me during my editorship of the campus newspaper at Wesley College concerns the author's responsibility to the text and moral questions surrounding anonymous and pseudonymous writing. The issue of whether responsibility is inherent in authorship is vital in a journalistic context but also has implications for critical study, communication, and with the concomitant redefinition of how information and/or literature is disseminated.

I feel Cornell University would be a stimulating place to continue my studies, and I look forward to studying with Coren Dale in connection with his work on Thomas Hardy. The interdisciplinary education I am receiving in the Master of Arts Program in the Humanities—including my thesis work this spring—will make me a particularly capable candidate to continue my studies at Cornell, and I am excited about taking the next step in my educational process.

COMMENT

The author takes a highly intellectual approach to his studies, and goes quickly and deeply into literary theory. Assuming that the ideas in criticism are used correctly, this applicant is certainly ready for work toward a doctorate. The essay specifically mentions Cornell and one of its faculty members.

SLAVIC

I now possess a B.A. in Russian, and am deeply interested in Russian literature. I completed courses on Dostoyevsky and Chekhov beyond the required nineteenth- and twentieth-century literature courses. Consequently, I have become particularly interested in the source of Dostoyevsky's spiritual inspiration portrayed through Father Zossima in *The Brothers Karamazov* and the interpretation of Gorky's and Chekhov's plays. I admire the way that Chekhov interprets life's daily episodes.

As a University of Arizona student, I spent six months in Smolensk, Russia, teaching English to Russian children in preschools as part of an experimental research project. After completing my B.A. in Russian, I returned to Smolensk as a regional administrator, and directed the same teaching program with twenty-four teachers in three preschools. During that time I helped the program expand to Rostov where I taught for one term. I have recently grown to love teaching because it is a learning process for me as well as my students.

Before enrolling in the Graduate College, courses I will complete that are not listed on my transcript include: another semester of fourth year Russian, a seminar taught in Russian on Tolstoy, a survey of twentieth-century Russian literature in translation, and a studio art class, as well as continuing work on my thesis.

At present, I have two main interests, one being Dostoyevsky and the way he deals with issues of faith and reason. Turn-of-the-century writers also interest me greatly. Over the two semesters of my senior year, I am working on a 50–60-page senior honor thesis, comparing Gorky's *Lower Depths* and Chekhov's *Cherry Orchard*. Specifically, I am examining the way these authors present socio-economic transformation, and how this kind of transformation affects the characters of the plays.

I look forward to exploring these interests and developing new ones both in my work towards a Ph.D. and later in an academic career.

COMMENT

This applicant is strongly interested in his field, and is going to be a very good teacher. He has spent a lot of time in Russia, and is probably very fluent in the language, though he does not say so. He has thought a lot about Russian literature, and he has ideas. He does not mention the university to which he is applying.

URBAN PLANNING

I graduated from Wellesley College five years ago with a B.A. cum laude in sociology. After graduation I worked as an assistant to an executive at a publishing firm. The position was interesting and I did a lot of problem solving for my employer, but it did not seem as if it would lead to anything. I was a glorified secretary, and I wanted to do something more. Last year I went to Perth, Australia, a country I had always wanted to visit. I found the air just as clear and the spaces just as wide open as I had anticipated.

For some time I have realized that I wanted a new career. I have put much thought into this and have decided to apply to the program in urban and regional planning at the University of Illinois at Urbana-Champaign. I feel that the computer skills I acquired at school and work, along with the statistics and demography I learned in sociology, will be a great help in urban planning.

I see urban planning as a discipline that achieves beautiful results and makes communities better places to live. The planner deals with many groups of people with differing values, and tries to attend to their interests, while also serving the community as a whole and preserving the land and the countryside.

I've traveled to the western states several times. I took a year off from college between my sophomore and junior years and worked in Los Angeles as a sales clerk in a photo shop and also was a volunteer at the Museum of Contemporary Art. I did a lot of walking around the city and thought about the lives of the people I saw on the streets. At the end of the year I realized I did want to get my bachelor's degree, so I returned to Wellesley for my last two years. As my grades show, I worked much harder during my junior and senior years. I also spent several months in France before college, living with a French family and learning to speak French.

When I have traveled I've seen how our culture has gone awry, in the smog haze, the strip malls, and the desert towns that look like scabs. I sometimes think we are coming close to destroying our world. I don't think that our rapaciousness makes us happy. It's impossible to believe that the commuters choking the freeways want to be there.

I think it's inertia and the lack of planning that keeps us stumbling along the same paths. I see urban planning as a possibility for change, a discipline that uses the knowledge we have to strive towards a new relationship with each other and with the earth.

My goal is a job working on urban and community planning in the public sector or in private consulting. I hope to work to help to create a more sustainable urban environment. The University of Illinois is particularly attractive to me, not only because of your program, but because of the location and your department's involvement within the region. I like the fact that your faculty members are engaged in research and public service and I look forward to taking courses with them in environmental studies, community development and transportation and preservation planning. The midwest is my home and I see its unique aspects. It combines big, sprawling cities like Chicago with small towns amid beautiful fertile country. I want to study in the environment where I will work. Please consider me as a candidate.

COMMENT

This statement does not say much about the applicant's intellectual development, but concentrates on her experiences and how they led to her decision. She has thought about urban planning, and has made a choice of field and location. This essay is directed specifically to Illinois. Incidentally, she notes how her grades improved after taking time off from college.

LAW

It was not until my senior year at Haverford that I decided to apply to law school. Once I made my decision I quickly became excited by it and the possibilities it opened up.

In pursuing a career in law I can follow an interest I have had since I was a boy—the environment. I was able to further my knowledge of the environment at Haverford College. As a history major with an environmental studies minor, I profited from classes in everything from specific, local environmental problems to international environmental policy. Not only did I learn more about the environment, I learned more about what I could do to protect and preserve it. I was particularly interested in classes on policy and law formation, both domestic and international.

During one of my terms off I worked as a research intern at the Environmental Institute, a non-profit research group located in Washington, DC. There I saw that getting a law degree would open doors to jobs where I could make an impact in environmental protection and policy. At EI I worked under lawyers who were working directly with different groups from around the world to solve their specific environmental problems, who worked to create environmental laws and standards in newly developing Eastern European governments. Others worked with small environmental groups in the U.S. to preserve specific ecosystems through legislation. This is the type of work that I would love to do. With my social science background this is the area where I can make the most difference. Environmental regulation involves complex issues, and I have learned that there are no quick or easy answers to these issues. I want to be able to work these problems out.

I want to go into law because I see that the law provides rules by which people can resolve differences on the basis of reason, fairness and predictability rather than brute strength or guile, and because it will enable me to work for the environment.

COMMENT

This applicant provides good reasons for his interest in law. His account of the influence of his internship is convincing; he seems to be a solid applicant. The only odd note is in referring to his social science background. He does not mention the university to which he is applying.

HISTORY

I am applying to the doctoral program in history at Indiana University. I have spent the last six years attempting to prepare for a career in academics, and feel that I have the necessary tools to successfully complete a doctorate and enter the academic profession. Upon the basis of correspondence, research, personal visits, and guidance from advisers at the universities of Wisconsin and Toledo, I believe that Indiana University offers all of the things I am looking for in a graduate program in history.

My research interests center around social movements in late Victorian and Edwardian Britain, and I am particularly interested in studying public reaction to naval reform. I toured your library graduate stacks and was amazed at the immense number of journals, newspapers, memoirs, and secondary literature available. I was so impressed with the British resources that I am in the process of obtaining an English Speaking Union travel grant to fund a visit to the university library to complete my M.A. thesis research at Toledo. If accepted, I would be interested in pursuing minor fields in South Asian, modern Continental European, and modern East European history as well as continuing a long-term research project on

Japanese-American immigration to northern Minnesota following the Second World War.

I am constantly working to improve my historical knowledge and have been able to set up directed reading tutorials with my adviser in British imperialism and modern British feminist theory in addition to independent study. Currently I am translating into English the diary of a Norwegian sailor impressed into the English navy during the Napoleonic Wars.

Since I decided to pursue history six years ago, all of my academic efforts have been spent preparing for the doctoral degree. As an undergraduate I received degrees in history and history of science and technology. I worked in a wide variety of fields which helped lay the groundwork for more specialized study. I am currently receiving more specific master's training in the major field of modern Britain and the minor fields of modern Eastern Europe and Russia and modern Germany. As an undergraduate I carried a 3.5 cumulative g.p.a. (on a 4.0 scale), 3.75 in history work, and 4.0 in history of science and technology. In my M.A. program I am currently carrying a 4.0 g.p.a. (60 credits), and in fact I have not received a grade lower than "A" in a history or history-related course since my sophomore year. Since graduating with my B.A., I have finished 78 credits and achieved a perfect 4.0 g.p.a. In addition to historical training I have also spent a year working as a graduate intern for the U.S. Department of Education. My responsibilities included tutoring, counseling, teaching and developing curriculum for the High School Upward Bound program, a federally funded program aimed at aiding first-generation, minority or low-income students to attend college. My specific duties involved traveling to inner city high schools and working with Hmong, Vietnamese, Hispanic and African-American high school students. This experience gave me a unique perspective on the wants and needs of an important segment of incoming undergraduate students.

I have received several academic awards and honors during my career. As an undergraduate I was awarded the Sigma Chi National Scholarship seven different quarters and made the University Dean's List four times. In 1993–1994 I was granted a Charles Phelps Taft

Minority Fellowship at the University of Toledo, a two-year award in which the first year is spent concentrating solely on course work and the second as a teaching assistant in the history department. I have also received a number of work-related and community service awards. I believe that it is at least as important to be a decent human being as it is to be a good scholar and teacher.

COMMENT

This applicant seems almost too good. In addition to her main field of 18th century Britain, she wants to minor in South Asian, East European, and Central European history, and has a long-term project on Japanese immigration to Minnesota. On top of this she is translating a diary from Norwegian into English. If everything she says is true, she is an exceptional candidate. She could have cut her essay to highlight her most important achievements; this would have given the department a sense that she is focused, as well as talented.

ENGLISH

I have spent the last year and a half here in Beijing, China, where I have been teaching, building close relationships with students and teachers, learning the language and about the culture, and ultimately learning much about myself. I came to China on a Fulbright grant to teach English and study Chinese culture. The original term of my grant was for a year, but I have found the experience to be so valuable that I decided to extend my stay for an additional year. My experience has been personally rewarding in many ways, and has been invaluable in shaping and focusing my academic interest in American literature and what it can tell us about America.

As a result of living in China I am more conscious of the cultural elements that constitute the idea that we label "America," ideas that, growing up as a second-generation Chinese-American, I too internalized and used in constructing my identity and what I have come to think of as an American character in general. These ideas associated with America are for example, those of unbounded space, limitless possibility, the Wilderness, the Frontier, and the power of the individual to shape his own world and his own destiny.

I would like to do research on the way the American writers have been influenced by and have addressed the ideology that has grown out of the American situation. As an English major I studied literary theory and the relation between signs and signifiers. But what if literary theory were applied to "America" as a text, or "American history" as a text? I would like to pursue research on the ways in which authors have read and interpreted the American situation and more specifically, the unique historical circumstance of America as the "New World" that provided the ideological basis not only for the building of a nation, but more importantly, for the construction of the self.

Primarily I am interested in doing research on the subversive elements of the American mythos, the insubstantial and illusory character of the American dream, and the misplacement of value in American life that leads to a spiritual and hence cultural impoverishment within a society of plenty. In particular, I would like to do research on the work of F. Scott Fitzgerald, who is most noted for his explicit address of these issues, but I would also like to study the work of William Faulkner and to show how these cultural and historical elements operate within his work as well.

COMMENT

This writer has clear ideas about what she wants to do, and seems to be well equipped to do it. The fact that she is Chinese-American (though she had to learn Chinese), had a strong and understandable effect on her thinking and on her goals. She includes enough references to literary theory to show that she is trained in the area. She does not mention the university to which she is applying.

RUSSIAN

I decided to concentrate on Russian literature fairly early in my undergraduate career. It was not a certain class or reading a certain text that led me to this decision, but the gradual recognition that the study of literature affected me more, both intellectually and emotionally, than my work in any other discipline. I find literature to be the most powerful way to explore basic human questions.

Once I had gotten a taste of Russian history, culture, and (most of all) literature, I was hooked. Initially, much of what I read was in translation, and the prospect of reading the masters of Russian prose and poetry in the original was too tempting to resist. Second language acquisition is a slow, steady process, but five years of study have given me a firm base from which to work. I also spent nine months in Moscow, during which I solidified my language skills and gained a clearer perspective of modern Russian life.

I have become particularly interested in the interpretation of Chekhov's stories. I have also researched and written about Christian symbolism in the psychology of Chekhov's *Black Monk* and the ideas in Dostoyevsky's *Crime and Punishment* of justice and mercy.

In my graduate studies I hope to continue building on a foundation started in the past few years. As a scholar, I try to have a broad approach, viewing things as a whole, looking for context and comparisons. This is reflected in the courses I have taken at college. In addition to my language and literature courses, I have studied the economies of Eastern Europe and Russia in a comparative economics class and a class on the political economy of transition. I have a solid background in Russian history, having taken courses on the history of Russia beginning in the 16th century and on Soviet history.

With a Ph.D. in Russian literature I hope to teach at the university level, develop my aforementioned research ideas and, thus, properly trained, make a significant contribution to the profession. I am also anxious to see the direction that modern Russian literature will now take amid such rapid, chaotic change.

COMMENT

This student seems to be well trained in Russian literature, and refers to his competence in Russian. He has also studied the Russian economy and wants to relate this to literature. He sounds like a good bet as a graduate student. He does not mention the university to which he is applying.

PSYCHOLOGY

While attending Mason State University I learned about Human Factors Psychology. I was excited to learn of a career in which I could study psychological issues in applied contexts such as human computer interaction and aviation psychology, two areas that have always been of keen interest to me.

To prepare for a Human Factors career I have taken classes in Calculus, Fortran, C, and Pascal, in addition to my undergraduate major in Psychology. When I graduate I will have participated in over three years of psychological research studying basic mechanisms of attention. I am currently working with Dr. Sawyer on a Senior Thesis research project in which we are studying repetition effects on negative priming. I plan to submit this research for publication next spring. I am also planning to participate in a human factors internship with a local company under Dr. Sawyer's supervision prior to my graduation.

My career plan is to become a researcher of HCI and display design in either academia or industry. My specific interests include the design of training and tutorial devices, and the role of spatial cognition in virtual environments. These interests seem to fit with the present programs of several faculty at the University of Wisconsin. Dr. Rogers' textbook on "Psychology in Engineering," especially chapters four and five, has helped me to solidify my areas of interest and my desire to pursue my graduate study at the University of Wisconsin. I thoroughly enjoyed the tech reports Dr. Roger's gave me on "Cognitive Issues in Virtual Reality" when I met with him and visited the University of Wisconsin campus this summer. I also enjoyed meeting with Dr. Katherine Sloane and discussing her areas of interest. From this visit I know that the Engineering Psychology program at the University of Wisconsin is one that I would be excited to have the chance to work with.

COMMENT

This applicant singled himself out as one who knew a lot about the program and was very interested in a particular area. He mentioned two faculty members that he met on a visit; if he is a borderline case they will probably support him. A slight problem is that one faculty member's name is either Rogers or Roger; the applicant doesn't use apostrophes correctly.

ENGLISH

When I finished my MAT at Pennsylvania in 1992, I accepted a teaching position on the Fort Towers Indian Reservation in north-central Montana and found myself immersed in a West of both legend and modernity, with the area's oldest inhabitants as my guides. I came to the West as a pilgrim and a student, with a unique combination of interest and education enabling me to understand and evaluate a people and their literature at a particularly opportune time.

The literature of the American West is experiencing an unprecedented surge of popularity. The currents run deep. A contemporary group of Western writers has begun the daunting task of recording and comprehending a past which is quickly waning. From Native American authors like James Welch to descendants of settlers like Ivan Doig, this flood of writing requires study and examination by critics with both passion and perspective for the material. It is into these waters that I intend to step.

My own research continues from the work I did at Pennsylvania on the British Romantics. One of the primary and rarely identified influences on many of the Western writers of this century has been and continues to be the British writers of over a century ago. British Romanticism, with its exploration of the ties between nature and inspiration, subject and object, has had a recognizable effect on the writings of Norman Maclean, Ivan Doig, Mary Clearman Blew, and others.

The connection between 18th and 19th century British writing and 20th century Western American writing is strongest in Norman

Maclean, who taught the writings of the British Romantics for forty years at the University of Chicago. In his most popular work, *A River Runs Through It*, Maclean suggests that nature and art are enough to provide solace in the face of human tragedy; however, when he revisits the question in his last work, *Young Men and Fire*, he seems far less certain. It is with this material and these questions that I intend to approach a project the length and breadth of a dissertation.

I am applying to Northwestern because I need a strong research facility with a diverse English faculty. While many departments offer instruction in British and American literature, few have any faculty working on Native American writers. Furthermore, my research has led me to the writing of Professor Ron Noel. Because of his work tracing the influence of the European Romantics on American Literature, Professor Noel will be essential to my efforts to delineate the Romantic issues of transcendence, subjectivity, beauty, and the divine in the literature of the modern West.

COMMENT

This writer has a clear idea of what he wants to do, and a convincing explanation of how he got interested. He mentions a professor who will be essential; he should only do this if he knows that the professor will be available for the next couple of years.

CHAPTER 7

TRANSCRIPTS AND REFERENCES

When I went to Rutgers I was Joe College. I cared more about the fraternity and chasing women than I did about course work. In my junior year I changed. I took a class in twentieth-century German history and found it almost impossible to understand the things that had happened. I knew then I wanted to go on and see if I could learn why this century was so bloody. I decided to get a graduate degree in modern history, but my grades were so uneven I was sure I couldn't get admitted to a first-rate school like North Carolina without good references.

—HUGH

TWO PARTS OF every application will be your transcripts and references. They are both sent in to the programs by other people, not by you, so there is plenty of room for mistakes and confusion. Getting the transcripts sent in is clerical work, but it has to be done right. Since they are a record of your past work, transcripts cannot be improved. As for references, there is a lot you can do to get good ones. In this chapter we'll tell you how.

TRANSCRIPTS

Every admission committee wants official transcripts of your grades from all the universities and colleges you have attended, even a school at which you took only one extension course.

Contact the Records Office of every school you have gone to after high school, and ask them to send transcripts to each program you are applying to. To avoid delays, telephone the institution first to find out how much each transcript will cost and mail a check to cover that with your request.

Johanna was working as a nurse when she began to think about improving herself. To start with, she took a Saturday morning course in health delivery systems at a Boston college, and a year later she enrolled in a class in nursing administration to see if she liked the challenges well enough to change to that field. She did. When she applied to graduate schools, she found out that she had to have transcripts from both those colleges, where she had taken only one class, sent to all the programs. She even needed a transcript from a math course she had taken at a local university when she was in high school. Each transcript was only a few dollars, but she applied to eight different programs, which added up.

Allow plenty of time for your records to be sent. Weeks after Johanna had sent in her applications, she received postcards from two of the programs telling her that they had not received transcripts from one of the colleges. She had to telephone that college again and ask to have the transcripts of her grades sent as soon as possible.

IF YOUR GRADES ARE BAD

If the transcripts are about to reveal that your grades are not very good, your prospects are not hopeless. This is something you must deal with in your essay. Was it because you weren't mature enough at that time to settle down? Perhaps you had a family crisis or had to pay all your expenses and supported yourself by working many hours a week. The essay is where you convince the faculty committee that you are different now and are committed to going ahead.

BE SURE EVERYTHING IS IN

Most programs will send you a card or a letter saying either that they have received all of the required material, or that some part is missing. The missing pieces are likely to be transcripts or letters of recommendation. If you do not hear from a university you are applying to, give the staff a reasonable amount of time to process your papers before asking whether your application is complete. They may have hundreds of applicants, and each one has the application form, test scores, transcripts and letters of recommendation that come in at different times. They are inundated with paper.

But if after weeks you hear nothing, it is a good idea to call or e-mail the programs well before the deadline to ask if they have received all the required material. Occasionally things do go wrong, and then all you can do is to make telephone calls to take care of this. Keeping on top of the situation can prevent a one-year delay in your education.

Most schools will not process your application unless all the material they asked for is there before the deadline. If the program gives out an e-mail address, you can use it for these inquiries. If you have access to it, e-mail is a fast and inexpensive way to ask questions or send information.

REFERENCES

All programs require letters of reference. These are important. An enthusiastic letter can give you an enormous boost. At least some recommendations must be from faculty members, because the committee wants to know how good a student you will be, and only other faculty can can tell them that. If you need additional references, find employers or people who know you professionally. It's best if they have some connection with the field. If you are applying for an M.S. program in computer science, a letter saying that you were a great youth counselor is not going to help much. Letters from friends or neighbors are almost useless.

Here is a letter a professor sent that helped a student get a $14,000 fellowship.

Thomas Burton is an honors student who is completing a four-year program in three years. Because his scores on the entrance examinations were so high, he did not have to take the beginning calculus courses and went directly into an honors third-term calculus. In his first year at the college his grades in mathematics and physics were A+, except for his physics laboratory for which his grade was only (!) an A. He also took a class in philosophy and for that received another A+.

Last year he took a sizable course load—quite a bit higher than most good mathematics honors students—and was rewarded with a rather extraordinary string of nothing less than A+s. He is clearly a very talented and clever student who has a great capacity for hard work. This year's result was of the same very high order and he achieved one of the best academic records of any student ever.

Tom was on the Mathematics Olympiad team in his last year at school, a great honor.

This year Tom was asked to teach a class, something few undergraduates are ever asked to do. I am delighted to be able to report that he did a singularly good job at it. He has very good rapport with students and they appreciate the efforts he makes for them.

He has a pleasant, though somewhat shy personality. He communicates well with others and would work well in a group. I believe he would be an excellent fellowship holder. He clearly has a great future in front of him and I have no hesitation in recommending him highly.

You do not have to be such a super student as Tom, who incidentally was offered fellowships at every university he applied to. Hardly anyone is that exceptional. No department expects all its applicants to be.

Here is a letter for a less impressive student.

I taught Mr. Warner in the course: Queen Victoria and the Victorians. This is an advanced seminar course, usually taken by graduate students, not undergrads like Bill Warner. It is a difficult course, and a good grade requires a thorough understanding of some advanced ideas. Mr. Warner did very well; his final grade was an A. His work was consistently good throughout the semester.

Mr. Warner is a reliable student and a stable person, perhaps a bit too shy to participate fully in class discussions, but his seminar paper was excellent. I know that he has some tutoring experience, and that he has received various academic awards and scholarships. He

*has a pleasant personality and it is easy to talk to him one-to-one. He
is a capable person, and I recommend him strongly for graduate study.*

HOW TO GET GOOD REFERENCES

What you want to do is to get as enthusiastic a recommendation as
possible. How can you get a really good reference? When you read
Tom's letter you realize that the professor knew him well. He includes details rather than generalities. If he had merely said that
Tom was brilliant, his letter would have much less impact.

When you read the letter recommending Bill Warner, you see
immediately that the writer did not know him very well. His knowledge apparently was limited to one class, and some conversation.
He uses phrases such as "thorough understanding," "did very well,"
and "consistently good." Only the seminar paper was excellent. Bill
Warner needed to single himself out. He should at least have provided the professor who was writing the letter a complete list of his
academic awards and scholarships, and listed his tutoring experience. Just by talking to the recommender, showing his enthusiasm,
and making sure that his achievements were known, he could probably have gotten a much better letter.

Almost no faculty member sets out to write a negative letter, but
sometimes a letter may be less than enthusiastic and damn the student with faint praise. This can easily happen, even if you are brilliant, if the writer does not remember you very well. The writers
can't mention your accomplishments without knowing what they are.
Be sure to tell them.

"OPEN" OR "CLOSED" RECOMMENDATIONS

You can ask to have "open" recommendations written for you, which
means that you can read the letter, if it is on file in your department
or in the placement office. However, this is not a good idea. Letters
are usually accompanied by a covering form that indicates if the
letter is open or not. The admissions committee knows that the
person writing the reference was aware that the student could read

it and so may not have felt free to give an honest opinion. If the recommender writes a flattering letter and the committee sees that it is open they tend to devalue it. It's far better to let the recommendations remain closed. If you are uneasy about what a professor might say about you, don't ask that person for a reference.

One thing you must never do is to send in a name as a reference without telling the person. If someone just receives a form with your name on it and a space for a recommendation, who knows what he or she will do? Or even if that person will remember you. Before you give someone's name for a reference, always ask for permission.

Start by contacting faculty members who taught courses in which you did well. Be sure to begin the process in plenty of time, at least two months before the deadline for application materials, and early enough in the term so that professors aren't racing to grade tests and term papers before the semester ends. As important as your letter is to you, it will probably not be number one on their list of things to do. They may put it off until they have time to think it over, a time that could be months in coming. You want to give potential recommenders plenty of information about yourself, and make it as easy as possible for them to write the letter.

You need references from people who know you and will stress your strong points, not like a letter sent in by a professor in China about a student who hoped to come to the United States.

In its entirety this letter read, "The only thing I know about Zhang is that he sat in my class all year with his nose dripping."

A SHORT RESUMÉ—A BIG HELP

Don't just walk into a professor's office and ask point-blank for a recommendation.

Instead, when you go to his office or contact him, give the professor a short resumé that includes some of your accomplishments. Mention the course you took with him, and tell him that you are going to ask for a letter. He may not remember much about you, but tell him that this sheet gives the basic facts, and spend a few minutes summarizing what you have done. You should give your recommender time to recall you instead of bringing up the request immediately. Then you might say, "I am applying to graduate school. Do you feel that you can write me a good letter of reference?" If the faculty member doesn't feel able to do so or does not want to write a good letter, this gives him the chance to decline, and saves you from having a lukewarm letter sent out.

This is better than walking in and springing the request on him and certainly far preferable to not asking at all. Also, if the professor wants to talk to you a bit in order to recall you better, the resumé gives a basis for a conversation. Faculty members often complain that students come into their offices without warning to request recommendations. They can't remember this person, and find out only by looking it up in the grade book that the student got an A in History 355 two years ago. This situation is very awkward for both of them.

MAYBE THE LETTER WON'T BE GOOD

Sometimes a person doesn't want to say to your face that he or she is reluctant to write a good letter, and will agree halfheartedly. You should be able to tell that this is not going to be a letter that will do you much good. You may have to rely on your instincts.

If you are worried about this, don't make the decision right then and there to ask for a letter. Tell the professor that you will send the necessary forms (these should be in your application packet) to be filled out. Later, think over all the conversations you have had with recommenders, choose the people you feel will write the best letters, and send them the forms. To the faculty members whom you are uneasy about, just send a short note saying that you will not need a recommendation after all. Both of you will heave a sigh of relief.

GET TO KNOW THE PROFESSORS

If you are are still in college, it should not be difficult to get faculty recommendations. Still, there are simple things you can do, either as an undergraduate or a graduate student, to single yourself out. Go to the professors' office hours even if you are doing well in class. Since you are interested in the subject, you should have questions to ask, or points to discuss. You want the faculty members to know *you* and to know your strengths, so that they will be glad to recommend you. Grades are important, but so is personal contact. If you are interested in the subject, it's natural to discuss it with your professors during office hours.

Single out one or two of your classes for special effort. Participate in class, and read the textbooks and class notes before class so you understand the new material and can ask informed questions. Try to understand the structure of the course, and how it fits into the field. If you show that you can do this, you will make a good impression.

Start writing term papers and other important assignments early enough to do a thorough job on them. This way you can go and talk to the instructor about the assignment while you are researching and working on it.

Ideally, when you ask for a recommendation the professor will know you, and you will have already talked about possible graduate schools. One of these may be the professor's old graduate school, and if he or she is willing to write a letter to that program, it will be a positive one. This letter is written to people who know the professor; his reputation for sending good students is at stake. The letter will be a great help to you.

Letters of recommendation are so important that you should consider applying to a school for which you know you can get a good letter. A professor may have close connections at some university. Maybe he or she got a Ph.D. there, or has sent several good students there, or has a colleague at that school. If such a faculty member encourages you to apply, push that school up a notch or two on your list. A strong letter from a respected faculty member who is known to the admissions committee can have a big impact.

This is not to say that you should pick your professor's alma mater if the program isn't what you want. The program you have the most enthusiasm for should be the focus of your efforts.

PROFESSORS WERE ONCE IN YOUR SHOES

Don't be shy about asking for references. Most professors are happy to oblige. They want their former students to do well, and are pleased if one wants to go to graduate school. And remember they, too, once asked for references. If they hadn't, they would not be professors today.

THE PLACEMENT OFFICE

Almost every college maintains a placement office, which helps its graduates in their job searches. One thing that office does is to handle letters of recommendation. A student can ask professors to send their recommendation letters to the placement office, where they will be kept on file. When the time comes, the placement office will send out copies of the letters to wherever the student requests. These documents are official and will be accepted by all programs. This makes it easy for a professor to write one carefully composed letter, saving the trouble of sending out letters and forms to various places.

OUT OF SCHOOL FOR YEARS?

If you graduated a few years ago, it may be more difficult to get recommendations from former professors. In the first place, you may have to make your request by phone or by mail.

What do you do? Most professors keep their grade books and can see what grade you earned in a class you took five or six years ago. That gives a professor a basis for a recommendation, but she may not remember much about you. The general principle is the same. Supply information about yourself, including all the most impressive facts, and tell her the name and date of the course you took before you request the recommendation. If the approach is by letter, you can supply all the information and say that you will telephone later to discuss the possibility of a recommendation.

If your first contact is by telephone, when you talk to a professor say that you will send a complete resumé. You probably shouldn't ask at that time if she will recommend you, as that puts her on the spot. You might say that you hope she can write a strong recommendation after seeing your material. After all, a telephone call from out of the blue is even more of a surprise for a faculty member than if you appear suddenly at her office. Assume that she may be willing to recommend you when she has seen the resumé; if she's not, she will tell you.

SEND A RESUMÉ WITH YOUR LETTER

Mail potential recommenders your resumé, along with a letter telling about yourself in which you describe what you have been doing. If you have been out of school for a few years, this letter is particularly important. Try to show that you have been accomplishing something worthwhile since getting a bachelor's degree, instead of just hanging out. Give all the necessary information about the type of recommendation you need and tell the professor where to send it.

Briefly tell about the program you are applying for, why you are interested and what work you hope it will lead to. You can send a copy of the personal statement on your application or write a concise paragraph, summarizing it. This will help the person writing the reference to produce a letter that emphasizes the same goals as your application. Most professors want to write a good letter for you; when you give them something to say, most of them will.

Follow up the resumé with another phone call to make sure the faculty member is willing to help you.

THE BEST REFERENCES

The best recommendation is a strong letter from a faculty member at the school to which you are applying. Members of the admission committee will hesitate to override the judgment of a colleague who has had personal contact with the applicant. Also, it is a bit awkward to tell a coworker that his or her candidate just didn't make the cut. If it is possible, you might even take a non-degree course in that program before applying for admission in order to get a good letter from the faculty member who teaches it.

WHAT HUGH DID

When Hugh started college as a freshman, he did not study and often turned in his homework assignments late. But by the time he graduated from Rutgers, he knew he wanted to work on a Ph.D. in history at the University of North Carolina. He also knew his grades were not good enough to get him admitted, but for personal reasons it had to be UNC.

He moved to North Carolina, got a job in a law office in Chapel Hill, and signed up as a non-degree student for an undergraduate course at UNC. He was serious and worked so hard that he impressed the young professor, who wrote an enthusiastic letter for him; he thinks this is the reason he was admitted. His plan worked, but he definitely had all his eggs in one basket.

GRADUATED LONG AGO

Johanna had worked for many years and wanted a better position, with more responsibility and a higher income.

When she graduated with a bachelor's and a nursing degree, she was glad to be through with college and to go to work as a nurse. She was not serious about her academic courses and never thought that one day she would want to go to graduate school. Ten years later she realized that she wanted to get a better position by becoming a nurse administrator.

She had graduated so many years earlier that many of her professors were no longer at her college. She had to hunt them down to get letters of recommendation.

Now that she wanted to improve her career prospects, she telephoned several faculty members who had liked her work and told them she would send a letter detailing what she had been doing. At first she was timid about asking busy professors to recommend her, but she realized that this task was part of their jobs. Johanna sent a detailed letter to each of them with a full account of what she had been doing since school, what she wanted from her graduate study, why she wanted to attend graduate school, and even sent them a copy of a newspaper article about herself and her work. She asked them to send the letters to the placement office at the college she had attended.

A LETTER TO A PROFESSOR

Unlike Johanna, who was remaining in the same field, some students want to make a complete change. Karen's undergraduate degree was in English, and she was aiming for a master's in landscape architecture. She, too, had graduated more than ten years earlier and had to hunt up some of her professors. When she found their current addresses, she wrote about what she had been doing since graduating. She also mentioned the classes she had taken with that faculty member and what in each course had remained with her. Here is one of her letters:

Dear Professor White,

As I said I would in our telephone conversation, I am enclosing my resume, which gives my employment history since I graduated ten years ago and moved to San Francisco.

At first I spent several years in offices with computers and engineers, lawyers and shoe retailers, and then some years in the catering business. Several years ago I earned my Professional Chef Certificate, and since then I have been self employed as a food stylist; that's the person who acquires the food, cooks and arranges it for advertising photography, both for still photographs and motion pictures.

I am not sure that I can apply all of these experiences directly to a career in landscape architecture, but I find many of the skills I have acquired over the years, such as computer literacy, confidence in business situations, salesmanship, and bookkeeping to be continually useful.

Working as a food stylist I've gained a lot of experience that will be directly applicable to Landscape Architecture. I work as a member of a team on creative projects. We begin each time with a specific goal, and through collaboration achieve a physical result. Every situation is unique. I use a well-practiced sense of shape, color, and space to combine the organic forms with the inorganic containers. I use problem solving skills every day. I am paid to look at things very carefully with an eye for both beauty and detail.

There are many things I enjoy in my work—it's a challenging job which demands creativity—but I've realized that I don't want to look back on a life spent selling frozen dinners and pop tarts.

When I took your class in Philosophy 145 I remember how you stressed that it was important for a person not only to satisfy his or her individual wishes but also to work to help the community. That is what I hope to do.

I began to search for a more fulfilling career a couple of years ago. I took extension courses in landscape architecture and in painting. I realized I wanted to work for a positive good but also to stay in a design field. My goal is to work in landscape architecture, to work with people and the environment.

Karen wrote similar letters to other former professors. Because she realized that it is difficult for professors to write enthusiastic letters if all they knew about her was that she got an A in a class taught ten years ago, she mentioned what there was in each of the courses that she had taken with them that had been important to her.

EMPLOYERS CAN ALSO HELP

If you graduated years ago, also ask your employers for letters of recommendation. In addition to former professors, both Johanna and Karen asked some of the people they had been working for.

They followed the same procedure, asking their former employers if they could give them strong recommendations, sending them short letters, telling about the programs they were applying to and giving them the address of the career placement office at their former universities. Those letters, too, became part of their official record.

Letters from employers show the applications committee that a student is reliable and works well. But be warned, many academics are not impressed by job experience so you can't rely only on such letters.

IF REFERENCES ARE NOT SENT IN ON TIME

One problem that sometimes occurs is when faculty members agree to write a letter of recommendation, but then put it off and don't get around to doing it. This is another reason for giving them a lot of information about yourself. It makes it much easier to write the letter if they have facts ready to put into it. Also, if they have on their desks a packet of information about you, they are more likely to write the letter than if they have only a scrawled reminder to "Write rec. for Fredholm." If that is all they have, they cannot do much more than hurriedly knock out something about Fred Holm.

Universities usually ask for three letters of recommendation, and on the application forms you have to list the names of the people you have asked. If you think you can get four positive letters, you can ask four people. This tactic has the advantage that if three of your letters come in on time, the department will probably process your application without waiting for the fourth. It makes it more likely that you will get three letters for your file, and saves you from the tricky task of nagging a letter writer who has not done the job. However, asking for more than four letters is not a good idea. Admission committee members are swamped, and don't like to read more letters than necessary. Also, the more letters you request, the more likely it is that one of them will be a lemon.

Occasionally a professor will ask a student to write a sample letter such as he or she would like to have sent in. If anyone tells you to do that, do it. It's hard to write a letter praising yourself, but this is an opportunity not to be missed. Forget about modesty, write a strong letter that will be a help to you, and send it to the professor, keeping your fingers crossed that it will be used as a basis for the final letter. Some faculty members will even copy the draft letter onto their stationery and send it off without alteration.

WHAT TO DO WITH RECOMMENDATION FORMS

A university will usually supply several identical forms for letters of recommendation along with the application blanks that it sends you.

Ideally what you want sent back, instead of just the forms with a few sentences about you written on them, is an excellent individual letter of recommendation, signed by the recommender, and stapled to the forms. You should fill in as much of each form as you can before you use it. At the very least you should include your name and the name and position of the recommender.

If you are using a college placement office that already has your recommendation letters on file, you can call the programs you are applying to and ask if they will accept a recommendation letter from the placement office without the form. If they say yes, which almost all will, all you have to do is to tell the placement office which letters to send and where to send them. It's a good idea to supply the placement office with stamped, addressed envelopes; in fact, some of them will require it.

However, some programs may demand that you use the forms. Then you have to send the forms to the placement office and request that the office match the professors' names on the forms with the letters on file for you, and send the forms and the letters to the programs you are applying to. The recommendation forms will not be signed, but these letters will be official, and every program will accept them.

If you are not using a college placement office, you will have to deal with each recommender separately. Give each professor who has agreed to recommend you a form for each program you are applying to, and ask him or her to write a full letter of recommendation and to send it, along with the appropriate form, to each program. This increases the chance of getting a separate letter, instead of only a couple of sentences scrawled in the space for recommendations on the form. Give the recommender stamped, addressed envelopes for the letters, clipped to the right forms, to increase the chance of getting them sent to the right places before the deadline.

You may not want the same letters sent to each program. For example, a professor has written a letter of recommendation for you to his old school. You want to use it there, but not at other schools. If you have four letters, you may want to send different sets of them to various schools. You can do this, but do it with caution. It's more complicated and, if the placement office is asked to mail out the references, the more complicated your request is, the greater the chance of error.

IN A NUTSHELL

Before you ask for a recommendation, prepare the way. Talk to the recommender, supply a resumé, tell or write good things about yourself. When you send the reference forms, also give your recommenders complete packets. These should contain:

1) addressed and stamped envelopes, so they can just write and mail their letters;
2) your letter in which you mention specific things about yourself that will single you out and recall you to mind;
3) copies of your resumé, even if the recommender already has one; and
4) copies of your grades if they are good; you can send an unofficial copy of your grades by just photocopying an official one.

If you follow these steps, you will get letters that are much better than the ones you would get if you don't. The letters are an important part of your application, and you can improve them by using simple and effective preparations.

CHAPTER **8**

GRADUATE
ADMISSION TESTS

> *I never do well on tests. I get so frightened. My hands feel like blocks of ice, my heart starts pounding, and my stomach begins to hurt. Then my mind freezes, and even though I know the answers and know that I do, I cannot seem to think of them when I am taking an exam. Soon after I leave the room I begin to recall the answers and know then what I should have said. If only I could get over this panic before I take the GRE.*
>
> *—OLIVER*

THE MOST FRIGHTENING part of applying to graduate school for many people is having to take the Graduate Record Examination General Test (the GRE) or an equivalent professional exam. But there is no way of avoiding it. Almost all graduate programs require that you take either the GRE or one of the professional tests, and have your scores sent directly to their offices. You may also have to take a GRE Subject Test in your field.

The first order of business is to find out exactly which tests you will have to take. The program's application material tells which test you need and often includes information on dates, locations, and how much it will cost you. Or you can contact the Educational Testing Service, which administers the GRE and GMAT (Graduate Management Admission Test). The LSAT is given by the Law School Admission Council, while the MCAT is administered by the Association of American Medical Colleges. The Miller Analogies Test, which is required by some programs, is administered by The Psychological Corporation. You can reach these organizations most easily using the Internet, as described their addresses are given in the Reference Addresses section at the end of the book.

The GRE and its relatives cause great anxiety, but a number of aids are available to help you out, including short courses, self-study guides, CD-ROMs, and books. Some of these are listed in the References section at the end of this book. Later in this chapter are sections on how to prepare, and on overcoming test anxiety.

The major tests cost up to $100 to take. The prices of preparation books range from booklets under $10 to large volumes with enclosed CDs that can cost up to $50. Full test preparation courses can cost $1,000.

THE GRE GENERAL AND SUBJECT TESTS

THE GRADUATE RECORD EXAMINATION GENERAL TEST

The GRE General Test is needed for most doctoral and master's programs and for some scholarships. It is designed to measure your verbal, quantitative and analytical abilities and is one of the ways schools evaluate how likely you are to do well in their programs.

Colleges differ very much, and the Educational Testing Service (ETS), which gives the tests, says that the GRE makes it possible for graduate committees to compare students from different undergraduate backgrounds. A GRE score of 600 means the same whether the student attended a small liberal arts college or a gigantic state university.

The General GRE takes several hours and is always scheduled in the morning. It is definitely not free. Both pencil-and-paper and computerized versions of the GRE are given, but the pencil-and-paper version is almost completely phased out. Each version has its pros and cons, which are discussed below. The test questions are changed regularly, so it's not much use asking friends who have already taken the exam to tell you the questions. The people who run ETS say that they are extremely careful to make all tests equivalent to each other. We have to take their word for this, though they are happy to explain in general terms how they do it.

WHAT EXACTLY IS THE GRE?

The general GRE has three parts, for verbal, quantitative and analytical ability. All of the questions are multiple choice, though in the future ETS plans to introduce essay questions.

The *verbal* part has four types of questions: antonyms, analogies, sentence completions and reading comprehension. The first tests your ability to select a word that means the opposite of the word given. For the second you have to pick out pairs of words or phrases that are related in similar ways; for example, "door is to wall as gate is to fence." For the third type you choose words that are logically and stylistically consistent to fill gaps in a given sentence. In the fourth, you read a passage and then answer questions about its meaning and ideas.

The *quantitative* part has two kinds of questions that test your basic mathematical skills, as well as your ability to reason quantitatively and solve problems. For this section you do not need any mathematics beyond what is usually covered in high school.

The *analytical* part tests how well you reason both analytically and logically. For example, you might have to choose, from several sentences, one that could be a logical explanation for a situation that is described.

The GRE is not an intelligence test and doesn't measure your creativity, perseverance, or motivation, all qualities that are important for ultimate success. It is supposed to be correlated with how well you will do in graduate school, particularly in the first year, but it certainly does not measure many important factors.

One thing to keep in mind—you have taken this type of test before, except for the analytical part of the exam. Only that time it was called the SAT or the ACT. Don't be surprised if your GRE scores are very similar to those other test scores.

WHAT ARE THE GRE SUBJECT TESTS?

The GRE Subject Tests are given in sixteen different subjects, including most of the fields you might study for an advanced degree, though there is no test in education. The format is similar to the

General GRE, but the questions require real knowledge of the subject. Each test is supposed to cover material that you would have learned working for a typical bachelor's degree with a major in that area.

If a subject test is required for your program, you can prepare for it in much the same way as for the general test, but the result probably depends strongly on the work you did in your major field. Bear in mind that the subject test assumes a broad knowledge of your major field. If you had a concentrated undergraduate education, don't be surprised to find large gaps in your knowledge. This is particularly true in the humanities.

In books listed in the References you can find samples of typical tests. Take one to see how well you do.

HOW THE SCORES ARE USED

Test scores give admissions committees a way to compare students from different colleges and different backgrounds. But the emphasis put on these scores can vary wildly from one program to another, and from one committee member to another within a program. Still, bad scores will hurt you, and good scores will help.

Colleges do not pay much attention to how well their own graduating students or their alumni score when they take the GRE. They don't tailor their courses or curricula so that their students will do well on these tests. If you come with excellent grades from a highly selective college, a poor result on the GRE may be discounted. But if your undergraduate school is not well known, the faculty committee evaluating applications will weigh the GRE more heavily.

WHAT THE FACULTY COMMITTEE LOOKS AT

Every section of the GRE has a maximum raw score, which is equal to the number of questions on the test, and it differs from section to section. These are converted to "scaled" scores, which have a maximum of 800 for each of the three sections. This scaled score is reported to you, and it always has zero for its third digit. But each section score is also reported as a percentile, which is the percent of test takers who did worse than you. The percentile scores are the important ones; they are the scores that the committee members use.

The raw scores and scaled scores don't relate exactly to each other, or to the percentile scores. On the quantitative section of the paper-based GRE, the maximum raw score is 60, which yields a scaled score of 800 and a percentile score of 97. But if you get a raw score of 57 you are still given a scaled score of 800, and a percentile score of 97. To put it another way, a student who gets 95 percent of the questions right receives the same scores as the student who gets 100 percent right. This is one reason why a difference of a few percentile points may not be taken seriously by committee members. The ETS publishes tables in their descriptive booklets that relate raw scores, scaled scores and percentile scores for each of its tests. The tables for the general GRE are derived from the scores of all of the people who took the test in a recent three-year period.

Scores that are below the 50th percentile are a serious handicap for an applicant. After all, these tests are taken by many people who are not strongly interested in graduate school, and many of them will end up doing something else. If you are not in the top half of this large group, you are not going to be a very attractive prospect. If you are interested in English, a score below 50 in the verbal section will be hard to explain away, but a poor score in the quantitative section of the test will not do much damage.

The way faculty members look at the scores also depends on the quality of graduate students they have been able to attract. The University of California at Berkeley and Harvard University have outstanding graduate students, and expect to attract more of the same. The M.S. program in Highway Drainage at Pavement College will admit almost anyone.

Experienced faculty members know that you cannot classify a potential graduate student on the basis of three numbers; human beings are more complicated than that. Still, outstanding scores (either way) will have an impact. Most admissions committee members think that there is not much difference between applicants whose percentile scores differ by less than 10 points. Scores in the 90th percentile, particularly the high 90s, are outstanding, in the 80s are good, in the 70s are merely okay, in the 60s are questionable, and in the 50s are a cause for concern.

Another thing to bear in mind is that in some tests it is impossible to score in the 99th percentile, because so many applicants get high scores. As noted above, you can't score above the 97th percentile in the quantitative section of the general GRE because the top three percent of all test takers get scores of 800. If you have a score of 800, you get a percentile score of 97 percent because you have a better score than 97 percent of the test takers. One of the worst offenders is the GRE Subject Test in mathematics, in which the top eight percent of test takers get the maximum score, so the highest percentile you can get on this test is the 92nd. It's not clear how the tests are scored, but it's not necessary to answer every question perfectly in order to get the top score of 800 on a GRE exam.

A few faculty members will follow rigid rules about cutting off admissions on the basis of test scores, but most of them will look at the whole picture your application presents.

If you have a good undergraduate record from a selective school, have enthusiastic letters of recommendation, and write a winner of an essay, GRE scores that are lower than you hoped should not sink you.

WHAT YOU HAVE TO DO

There are differences between the GRE and the other tests, but for all of them you have to:

- register to take the test in plenty of time;
- pay the fee with a check, credit card or money order;
- show up for the examination at the time scheduled;
- present one photo ID with your signature (you must present a second ID if the first is questioned); and
- present your admission ticket.

Register early in order to get a testing site close to you, especially if you don't live near a big city. After you register you will receive an authorization voucher and be told the scheduled date, place, and time. Check your name and address and the other information to be sure it is accurate. If not, notify ETS immediately and request a correction. It takes a minimum of two to four weeks for the papers to get to you by mail. The voucher will be good for one year from its issue date.

Find out from the schools their deadlines for receiving your scores. Occasionally they are different from the date your application is due. ETS says that it sends out the scores 10 to 15 days after the test, but you had better allow plenty of time.

Some schools will be lenient if your scores do not arrive on time, and will begin to process your application without them. Others will shuffle you to the bottom of the pile if your application is not absolutely complete. They will probably send you a notice saying that they have not yet received your scores.

If your program requires, in addition to the general test, a subject test in your field, it will be scheduled in the afternoon. If you need one, find out the dates and locations. You can register for both tests at the same time.

There is a fee for each examination, which you can pay with either a check, money order, or credit card when you register. You can also sign up by telephone with your credit card. This fee covers the cost of sending the results to up to four programs. Your test scores are good for five years. ETS will send them (for a fee) to as many additional schools as you request.

On the day of the test, in order to be admitted, be sure to bring your authorization voucher and photo ID. It should be a government-issued ID such as a driver's license or a passport. You may be photographed at the test center if your identification is questioned.

PENCIL-AND-PAPER GENERAL GRE, AND SUBJECT GRES

The paper-and-pencil general test has seven sections that are timed separately. You are allowed 30 minutes for each. Only six of the sections are counted toward your grade; the other is a way for ETS to try out questions that might be used in the future. However, you don't know which section won't be counted. The number of questions per section varies from about 25 to 38, giving you roughly one minute per question. Your score is determined solely by the number of correct answers, or as ETS says, the "best" answers, which seems to indicate that there can be a best answer even if there is no correct answer. Nothing is subtracted from your score if you answer incorrectly, which means it is always better to guess at an answer than to leave a question unanswered.

Go through the whole test section, answer the questions you are sure of and skip those that are causing you trouble. Then go back to work on the ones that you left blank. Since you had trouble the first time around, it's not a bad idea to reread the questions carefully.

You indicate your answers by blackening ovals on an answer sheet. A common mistake is to mark the answer in the wrong column of the answer sheet. There are always five possible ovals to blacken, but some questions have fewer than five possible responses.

The Educational Testing Service has been phasing out the pencil-and-paper GRE, but the subject tests, given in the afternoons, will continue to be paper-based. They would be much more expensive to computerize than the general test, because it requires a lot of specialized knowledge to prepare them, and they are taken by far fewer people.

GRE ON THE COMPUTER

Most people will take the general test on computers. ETS calls it the Computer Adaptive Test (CAT), and it is quite different from the paper-based test.

The test is preceded by a tutorial that teaches you how to use the computer for this test. ETS says that you will find the system very easy to use, even if you have no computer experience. But people who have experience with a mouse and scroll bar will probably be able to move through the test faster and more effectively than those who don't. There is no time limit for the tutorial, and you can return to it during the test. But during the test, any time you spend rereading the tutorial will use up your test-taking time. If you are a returning student who has not been using computers, you should get some practice. Your public library probably has computers available.

DIFFERENCES BETWEEN THE VERSIONS

Three major changes were introduced with the CAT. First, you can't skip a question and return to it later; second, wrong answers count against you; and third, the questions that the computer gives you depend on how well you have been performing. The ETS implies that your score on a paper-based test will be roughly the same as on a CAT, even though the CAT seems more formidable. However, by the time you read this there will probably be no choice; you will have to take the CAT.

The words "computer adaptive" mean that the computer selects questions of varying difficulty for you, depending on how well you are doing. If you answer a question correctly, the following question will be more difficult; if your answer is wrong, the computer will ask an easier question next. Hard questions give you more points than easy ones.

Unlike the paper test, wrong answers can reduce your score. Since you can't skip a question, you may have to guess to get to the next question, but you should eliminate as many possibilities as you can before making your guess. The ETS does not say exactly how the CAT is scored. However, it does reveal that the score for each section is based not only on the difficulty level of the questions you have answered correctly and the number of correct answers, but the total number of questions you have answered in that section. The ETS advises specifically that if you are running out of time at the end of a section, you should guess on the remaining questions. But it also says that random guessing throughout the test could reduce your score. Since you can't skip any question, the ETS seems to be saying that you should guess intelligently during the test, but if you are really pressed for time, you should finish the section with random guesses.

This may be because random guessing early in the section will lower the difficulty level of questions you are asked, and therefore reduce your score. According to the Kaplan organization, a major test preparation company, your score is based on the difficulty level of the questions at which you get 50 percent right, and the number you get right is not as important as this level.

The three sections of a typical computer-adaptive general GRE might take two and one-quarter hours and have more than ninety questions. But in addition there may be two more sections, an "unidentified pretest section" and an "identified research section," which the ETS uses for test preparation. Your scores on these will not affect your reported score, but there may be four or five sections on the test. There is a one-minute break between test sections, and a ten-minute break midway through the testing session.

If you want, you can have a display on the screen of how much time you have left. This lets you pace yourself to finish the test without having to guess randomly at the end. The tutorial shows you how to get this display.

A big advantage of the GRE on the computer is that you get your scores as soon as you finish the exam; you know immediately how well you have done. After you see your scores, before you leave the testing center, you can choose the four institutions where you want the results to be sent.

YOU CAN HAVE THE TEST THROWN AWAY

If you feel that you did not do well, *before* you see your scores, you can have the test and its results canceled and discarded. Your fee will not be refunded. Once you see the scores, you cannot ask to have this done.

Whether or not you ask to have your scores canceled, you can retake the CAT to try to improve your scores, but not for at least sixty days. If you take it before this period your scores from the retake will not be reported and your test fees will not be refunded.

Also, if you asked for your scores to be reported, your earlier scores will be reported. There is no restriction on how soon you can retake the paper-based test.

PREPARATION

Don't wait to prepare. Get materials concerning the test from: Graduate Record Examinations, Educational Testing Service, P.O. Box 6000, Princeton, NJ 08541-6000. You want the current Information and Registration Bulletin and the General Test Descriptive Booklet; they are free. You can also use the Internet to order them.

The first booklet contains registration information, test dates and locations, and gives a lot of general information about the test. The second describes the test, and includes a sample test that you can take. It's a good idea to have someone else administer this test to you. When you do this, pretend it's a CAT; don't skip and don't look back. You get a little bit of the flavor of the real thing, and you can't cheat on the timing. It will tell you a lot about how much you should prepare for the real GRE.

You should become completely familiar with the instructions and the kinds of questions you will be asked. Pay particular attention to the types of questions that you are not accustomed to. For the CAT you should be familiar with computers; on the reading comprehension questions you will have to scroll through the text as you read the paragraphs you will be questioned on.

You can buy practice test books from the Educational Testing Service at many book stores. Some of the titles are listed at the end of this book. Buying and using these books is a reasonable level of preparation, but requires a lot of self-discipline. If you want to go all out, you can move to a higher level of test preparation.

MORE PREPARATION

The *New York Times* has said that ". . . coaching for tests is as much a part of the admission process as interviews." Several organizations offer further test preparation. The two that are best known are

The Princeton Review and the Kaplan organization. Others are Cutts Graduate Reviews, Prep Master Review, and Prep Doctor.

Courses you pay for, such as Kaplan's or The Princeton Review, are more expensive than buying books. The standard Kaplan GRE preparation course costs about $800. It includes a complete set of books and other preparation materials, an initial diagnostic test, and seven three-hour class sessions. These are followed by a final test and a final test review.

The Princeton Review offers similar preparation courses. You spend fewer hours in class, but also spend time in workshops and take four actual tests. Software is included with the course, which will cost you about the same as the Kaplan course. Both Kaplan and The Princeton Review offer classes in all large cities and near the campuses of major universities.

Cutts Graduate Reviews offers tapes and other materials for the GRE for under $200, while Prep Master says that its preparation is cheap and effective.

The ETS says that it doesn't do much good to prepare for the GRE, but you won't be alone if you opt to buy books and take preparation courses. You should certainly prepare enough so that the mechanics of the test are automatic for you, and the question styles are completely familiar.

If you go through a couple of sample tests, you will gain confidence, because you will know what to expect in question styles and time limits. But keep in mind that the actual test will be different, since you will probably be taking a computer adaptive test.

Both the Kaplan organization and The Princeton Review say that their courses will definitely increase your scores in any of the graduate admission tests. The Princeton Review claims an average GRE score improvement of 212 points (out of 2400), and the Kaplan organization makes similar claims. This is a substantial increase, but it's hard to see where they got the number.

INFORMATION ON THE INTERNET

Much information about the tests, as well as sample tests and sales pitches for exam preparation courses, is available on the Internet.

The Internet will give you the GRE testing dates and sites, descriptions of the parts of the exam, and lists of books to help you prepare.

Currently the CAT is given three times a month in September through January, and once a month in the other months. The paper-based test is only given three or four times a year.

At the least, test yourself with practice exams to see how you would do if you were taking the GRE that day, and get to know the types of questions. You want to be prepared so you don't panic when you walk into the testing room.

TEST ANXIETY AND HOW TO DEAL WITH IT

Some people become acutely anxious at the prospect of taking tests. They get so panicky that they have difficulty with the questions even when they know the answers.

If you become terrified when you have to take an examination, you can take steps to lessen test anxiety:

1. Familiarize yourself with the types of questions you will be asked well before the exam. The more you have prepared yourself for this, the better you will do. Review what you know in good time. Don't try to cram the night before the exam, but get a good night's sleep.

   You should at least buy practice test books for the GRE General Test or the subject tests from the Educational Testing Service. As discussed above, several organizations, including The Princeton Review and the Kaplan organization, advertise books and classes to help you prepare for the examinations. Many people find the courses an excellent source of information and extremely helpful in getting them ready for the tests, but of course they take time and cost money.

2. On the day of the test, avoid caffeine and panicky people. Put your books aside and eat a moderate breakfast or lunch before the exam. If you are afraid you will get so anxious you will have difficulty functioning, stay away from nervous acquaintances. Panic is contagious.

3. Get to the exam room a few minutes early so you can familiarize yourself with the place and set out any supplies. When the test starts, read the instructions over twice and make sure you understand the questions before you plunge in; note what is important. If you don't understand something, ask the proctor as soon as possible. If you are taking the computer adaptive test, take plenty of time with the tutorial to be sure you understand how to use the computer effectively. If you have to write an essay, take a few minutes to organize your thoughts, make a brief outline and start off with a summary sentence. Keep working steadily, and even when time starts to run out, don't speed up.

When the test is over, don't torture yourself by thinking of all the mistakes you made.

If test anxiety is really bad and is hurting your performance, try to get counseling. A counselor on campus may be able to help you with this, either in workshops or individually. In a short time, he or she will be able to show you how to cope with this panic. If you are not a student now, see if you can find a counselor to help you.

A counselor probably won't tell you to relax completely, and you don't want to, not while you are taking the examination. You want to be calm but not too calm. A little stress is all right; it will make you alert and enable you to perform well. It's not good to relax so much that you sit in the room serene, happy and relaxed, not answering the questions and not caring how you do on the exam.

SPECIALIZED TESTS

If you are interested in a professional school, usually you will be required to take a specific test that measures your qualifications for that field. The format is similar to the GRE. Information about these tests, including dates and places, is also available on the Internet. The names of required examinations for some professional programs, and the relevant addresses are given below; also see the Reference Addresses.

GMAT

For a degree at a school of business, the required examination is the Graduate Management Admissions Test (GMAT). It is run by the Graduate Management Admission Council, which has representatives from 121 graduate schools of management. The test is administered by the Educational Testing Service in Princeton, N.J. For general inquiries, the address is: GMAT, Educational Testing Service, P.O. Box 6103, Princeton, NJ. The telephone number is 609 771-7330. The Internet site with the best information on the test is http://www.gmat.org.

This test is now given in computer adaptive form. It is designed to measure general verbal, mathematical, and analytical skills that are associated with success in the first year at graduate schools of management. It includes sections on mathematical skills that measure how well you understand concepts and can reason and solve quantitative problems and interpret graphic data. The verbal sections test your knowledge of standard English and measure how well you evaluate complicated writing.

The GMAT is given four times a year, in January, March, June, and October. It has three sections, verbal, quantitative, and analytical writing. The verbal and quantitative sections are scored in the range of 0–60, the analytical writing section in the range of 0–6. A total score in the range of 200–800 is given, based on a combined scaling of just the verbal and quantitative sections. All four scores are reported.

The GMAC itself offers preparation materials. The lowest level is *The Official Guide for GMAT Review*, or you can buy "Powerprep" software. Use the Internet address given above, or telephone 800 962-6740, to order their products.

The Princeton Review offers preparation for this test that consists of five three-hour classes interspersed with six three-hour workshops. The course also includes four actual GMAT exams.

The Kaplan course has six three-hour classes, a beginning and final practice test, and a three-hour final test review. Three extra help workshops are available. You can make up for missed classes with videos. These courses both cost about the same and are in the same range as the courses for preparing for the GRE.

LSAT

The LSAT is offered by the Law School Admission Council (LSAC) with the cooperation of American College Testing, of Iowa City. Prospective lawyers can contact the council at Box 2000, Newtown, PA 18940-0998; tel: 215 968-1001. The e-mail address is lsacinfo@lsac.org. The web site for the LSAC, at http://www.lsac.org, has free information and some LSAT preparation materials. For full information you need the *LSAT & LSDAS Registration and Information Book*.

The LSAT is a half-day standardized test required by all 194 law schools in the U.S. and Canada that are members of the LSAC, and about 35 that are not. It is given in February, June, October, and December.

It consists of five 35-minute sections plus a 30-minute writing sample. Each section has about 25 questions. With one 10–15 minute break after section III, the test takes close to four hours. The writing sample is not graded, but is sent to all the law schools that you apply to for them to use as they see fit. The reported score is given in the range of 120–180. You can retake this test, and the LSAC publishes statistics showing that most, but not all, people do better the second time.

Just four of the five sections contribute to your score; the fifth is used to compare this exam with others to make sure that all exams are equivalent, and to try out new questions for later use. However, you are not told which section does not count.

The test is designed to measure how well you comprehend, evaluate, and organize complex information, and also how well you reason analytically and logically. There are three types of questions, involving reading comprehension, analytical reasoning, and logical reasoning. Each section consists entirely of one type of question. In one test, of the four sections that counted, two were on logical reasoning, and one was on each of the other types, but the makeup of the test can vary. The questions can be quite difficult, and you should certainly spend some time and effort on preparing for all sections.

There are, as usual, various levels of preparation for this test. The LSAC offers eleven past tests for sale. A better deal is *The Official Triple Prep Plus with Explanations*, which contains three old tests with explanations of the answers, plus 50 writing sample topics used on former exams.

The Kaplan preparation course has eight three-hour sessions plus two practice tests. Three extra-help workshops are available. The Princeton Review preparation course consists of sixteen two-and-one-half-hour classes, plus four actual LSAT exams. These cost around $1,000.

MAT: THE MILLER ANALOGIES TEST

This is a test required for some programs in education and related fields. It is administered by The Psychological Corporation, 555 Academic Court, San Antonio, TX 78204-2498, tel: 800 622-3231. It is short and intensive. The test takes 50 minutes and has 100 questions, all of the type: "word A is to word B as word C is to word D." You are given three of the words, and must select the fourth from a number of alternatives.

The Psychological Corporation says that "fluency in the English language, a broad knowledge of literature, philosophy, history, science, mathematics, and fine arts, and the ability to reason out relationships may contribute to performance on the MAT." The test covers a great deal of ground in a short time. You not only have to know the meanings of all the words given, but also to have a lot of general information. In the *Candidate Information Booklet*, which you should send for, some sample questions are included. To do these correctly, you have to know, or guess, such facts as that limestone is a sedimentary rock, Spenser was a poet, and a neutral solution has a pH of 7.

In this test your score is based only on the number of correct answers. In effect, answers left blank are scored as wrong, so it is always to your advantage to guess. If you decide during the test that you are doing badly, you can exercise the "no score" option. No score will be reported, and no reportable record will exist that you have taken the MAT.

MCAT

If you are interested in medical school, the exam you need is the Medical College Admission Test (MCAT), which is offered only twice a year. It is administered by the Association of American Medical Colleges (AAMC). This test is a major hurdle for prospective medical students. You can't be a doctor without doing well on this test.

For information from the Internet, search under "MCAT," or look at the site http://www.aamc.org/stuapps/admiss/mcat/ to get information. The phone number for the MCAT Program Office is 319 337-1357. The address is P.O. Box 4056, Iowa City, IA 52243. Ask to be sent a copy of the announcement of the examination for the current year. It discusses fees, registration information, procedures for taking the test, and score reporting. It tells you everything you need to know about the mechanics of taking the test, and even gives some sample questions. It is free.

The MCAT has four parts. It's a standardized multiple choice exam, except for a writing sample. One part tests your verbal reasoning ability. Two others measure your knowledge of biological and physical sciences by posing scientific problems and asking you for the solution. Each of these three parts is scored on a scale from 1 to 15. Two 30-minute essay questions conclude the examination. They are on specific topics and measure how well you develop and synthesize concepts, and how clearly and logically your writing presents your ideas. The writing score is on an alphabetical scale ranging from J (low) to T (high).

The morning begins with an 85-minute test of verbal reasoning with 65 questions, followed after a 10-minute break by a 100-minute test on physical sciences with 77 questions. After a one-hour lunch break, you have 60 minutes to produce two writing samples, followed after a 10-minute break by a 100-minute biological sciences test with 77 questions. Almost six hours of tests make for a stressful day. The MCAT is supposed to be a test of your thinking skills as well as your stock of information. If you are in a premedical program, you should certainly talk to your premed adviser about this test and other aspects of the admission process.

Even if you are supremely confident, you should probably prepare for this test. One way is to use the preparation materials that are sold by the AAMC itself.

Both the Kaplan organization and The Princeton Review sell much more elaborate preparation courses. The Princeton Review course consists of eighteen three-and-one-half-hour classes plus four practice MCAT exams. The Kaplan course has eleven three-hour classes plus ten three-hour workshops, and three longer sessions devoted to practice tests and diagnosis of your performance. You can take up to four more practice exams. Both courses cost around $1,000.

DENTAL ADMISSION TEST

Prospective dentists need to take the Dental Admission Test. Given twice a year, it takes half a day and is in four parts: natural sciences (primarily biology and chemistry), reading comprehension, quantitative ability, and perceptual ability. You can get additional information from the Department of Testing Services, American Dental Association, 211 E. Chicago Ave., Suite 1840, Chicago, IL 60611-2678, tel: 312 440-2689.

OPTOMETRY ADMISSION TEST

This test is given twice a year by the Optometry Admission Testing Program. It measures academic ability and scientific knowledge. For more information, contact the Optometry Admission Testing Program, 211 E. Chicago Ave., Suite 211, Chicago, IL 60611-2678, tel: 312 440-2693.

PHARMACY COLLEGE ADMISSION TEST

This test is administered by The Psychological Corporation, 555 Academic Court, San Antonio, TX 78204-2498, tel: 800 622-3231. It is designed to measure general academic and scientific knowledge and includes sections on verbal and quantitative abilities, reading comprehension, and understanding of biology and chemistry.

VETERINARY COLLEGE ADMISSION TEST

If you are a future veterinarian, you need to take the Veterinary College Admission Test, which measures your knowledge of biology and chemistry, as well as your reading comprehension and verbal and quantitative abilities. The veterinary colleges you are interested in can give you information, or you can contact the Psychological Corporation, 555 Academic Court, San Antonio, TX 78204-2498, tel: 800 622-3231, which has designed and administers the test and will send you a copy of the VCAT Announcement. This material contains information about what is on the test as well as application procedures.

CHAPTER 9

YOUR CHOICE— WHERE TO GO?

> *It seemed like a long time to wait, but then I began to get acceptances from the different schools I had applied to. I wasn't accepted by all, but three offered me financial aid, and it was not easy to decide which to choose. Each one had something in its favor. Fortunately, I had until April 15 before I had to let them know.*
>
> **—ALAN**

IF YOU ARE admitted to the graduate program that is your first choice, and money isn't a problem, congratulations! You can skip the rest of this chapter. Or if you applied to only one, like Max, who made up his mind that it would be the University of Illinois architectural school for him or none at all, then when you are accepted, your decision is made for you. But if you are not completely certain which school to choose, read on.

LETTERS FROM THE PROGRAMS

Several weeks after you apply, you will begin to hear from graduate schools. First you will receive form letters or postcards saying that your application is complete, or that certain specific items have not arrived.

Later, you will get the letters you are waiting for, the ones telling you whether or not you are accepted. If you are admitted to several programs and don't know which one to choose, you are in a good position, far better than if you aren't admitted to any.

Now it is up to you to make the best decision.

YOUR ANSWER DUE APRIL 15

Almost every program has a standard date, April 15, by which you must notify the department that you accept its offer for the fall semester. Almost every major university has signed an agreement to abide by this date. That is, offers are held open until April 15, and schools will not require an earlier decision. The offer will usually be withdrawn if you don't send in your decision by that date.

On the other hand, there's no point in sending in your acceptance early if you are still waiting for decisions from other programs. You can even fax your acceptance at the last minute. As the deadline approaches, a nationwide flurry of telephone calls begins. Some programs will not have enough acceptances, and will be making telephone offers at the last minute. You may have been put on a waiting list, or you simply may not have heard. It's even possible that you will be made an offer by a program that has already rejected you. Cornell Medical School had 30 too many acceptances one year; they might have 30 too few some other year. Stay close to your telephone in the few days before April 15; it's a long shot, but you may get a better offer.

The agreement about an April 15 deadline was created by the Council of Graduate Schools, and is called the Resolution Regarding Graduate Scholars, Fellows, Trainees and Assistants. It is supported by over 350 graduate schools in this country, including every substantial program. The resolution is printed in full on page 247, together with the list of supporting institutions. The agreement contains these sentences: "Acceptance of an offer of financial aid (such as graduate scholarship, fellowship, traineeship, or assistantship) for the next academic year by an actual or prospective student completes an agreement which both student and graduate school expect to honor. In those instances in which the student accepts the offer before April 15, and subsequently desires to withdraw, the student may submit in writing a written resignation of the appointment at any time through April 15. However, an acceptance given or left in force after April 15 commits the student not to accept another offer without first obtaining written release from the institution to which a commitment has been made."

Some programs will try to get your decision before the deadline; they may say that the offer is withdrawn as of March 15. They are trying to fill their quota by "rolling admissions," pressuring applicants to commit themselves by an earlier date so they can send out more offers if they don't have enough acceptances. This conflicts with the agreement, but some departmental officers may not even know that there is such a thing.

If this happens, you can accept the offer and decline it any time before April 15 if something better comes along. This is not a nice thing to do, and you should not accept any offer unless at that time you expect to honor it. But the resolution says clearly that you may submit a resignation at any time through April 15. A department that demands an earlier commitment is violating the letter of the agreement. If one does this, you can accept its offer and decline it later without feeling guilty. In your letter declining the offer, you should mention that the department's institution supports the agreement.

To be fair, this agreement puts a small department at a disadvantage. If it has funds for four new teaching assistants and fellows, it is afraid to make five offers; if all five accept, they will be 25 percent over budget. If it makes four offers and waits until April 15 for the result, it may be scratching around in the reject pile for one or two TAs after all of the most promising students have committed themselves to go elsewhere.

A bigger program has more flexibility. If it needs ten new TAs and fellows, it can make twelve or fifteen offers, depending on past experience of the ratio of acceptances. It will try quite hard not to get too many, and can vary the intensity of its recruiting effort as the deadline approaches. If you get telephone calls on April 14 trying to recruit you, you know the callers don't have enough acceptances. If a program ignores you and is slow to respond to any last-minute question of yours, it might not mind if you went elsewhere. But in any case, a department has to honor the offers it makes.

Program officers see every kind of behavior. Most applicants are courteous and reliable, but some are not. Sometimes applicants will simply not respond to an offer; more rarely someone will accept an offer, and then decline it after the April 15 deadline. Once in a great while an applicant will accept an offer and then not show up at the beginning of the term. After a flurry of phone calls, his mother is located and says that he has decided to spend a few months seeking enlightenment in Katmandu. There is not much the program officer can do about this except to get mad as hell, but it's best not to go around leaving large black marks on your reputation.

WHAT ABOUT FINANCIAL AID?

Read the letters of acceptance carefully to see what they do not say as well as what they do. Is the offer absolutely clear on how much financial aid, if any, the program will give you and what part of the tuition and fees will be waived? One school may offer assistantships at a higher salary than another. But read both letters again. Does the assistantship also take care of your tuition? If you have to pay for tuition and fees out of your graduate school salary, that makes a big difference. Find out exactly how much you would be responsible for paying.

An offer of financial aid depends very much on your field and on your program. Law students typically do not receive much financial aid, nor do M.B.A. students. The trade-off is that they can earn big salaries after they have their degrees.

In an academic department, a science such as physiology or physics, or one of the humanities such as history or Spanish, where both a master's and a doctoral degree are given, more financial aid is generally awarded to students working on their doctorate than to master's candidates. Master's degrees take only between a year and three years, and often increase the employability and income of the people who have them. Since much more time is needed to work for a doctorate, master's students can finance their own graduate study more easily than doctoral students, who may spend many years working toward the degree. And faculty members in those departments are more interested in doctoral students, whom they get to know better.

Because it is more difficult to get support for a master's degree, if you are undecided whether to aim for the doctorate or an M.A. you might apply for the Ph.D. program and make your final decision later. Some people decide they have had enough and leave with the master's. There is no penalty for changing your mind.

ASSISTANTSHIPS AND FELLOWSHIPS

Faculty committees want to get the top students. They compete with other universities for the students that they judge are the most promising. If you are offered a fellowship for a fixed number of years, that means the committee thinks you have a lot of potential.

Some universities will send a letter saying you are admitted, but you will be notified about financial aid later. Then you have to wait to see what they offer you. They should make their offer by April 15. Before that date you can call the department to try to find out what your chances are. Someone may tell you if you are on a waiting list for financial support, but you probably won't get much useful information. If April 14 arrives with no word, call the Graduate Adviser and say that you were told you would be notified. Ask if you are getting an offer of financial aid. It is possible that the office is disorganized, or the letter is late, or your documents got misplaced in the flood of paper. You don't want your career to be derailed because of a lost letter.

The possibility of a teaching assistantship is better in departments that do a lot of undergraduate teaching, such as English, political science, and mathematics. If you are awarded an assistantship, and you do well, you can expect to keep it for several years. If you plan to go to graduate school in one of these subjects, you have a strong possibility of receiving financial aid.

Different departments use different strategies. One may give large fellowships to a small number of very desirable students. Another may offer smaller fellowships to more students or award relatively small fellowships but use them to increase the income of selected

TAs. Up to a point, departments can package their fellowship and TA funds in any way that they want. But they must have enough TAs to carry out necessary teaching. If you are planning to work on a Ph.D., and a department offers you money, that's a pretty good sign that the faculty want you, and you will start your graduate work known as a student with a lot of promise.

A department may put you forward for a university fellowship. These awards are often more prestigious than other fellowships, and the department may be competing with other departments for the funds. You may be offered a departmental fellowship only to have it replaced with a university fellowship if the department gets the funds. University fellowships are sometimes targeted for women or minority students, but not always. If you are offered a fellowship for which there is universitywide competition, that's a very good sign.

IF MONEY ISN'T MENTIONED

If a letter says, "Congratulations, you are admitted," but nothing at all about financial aid, don't think the department has forgotten to mention any money you will get. You can telephone to ask if it will give you support, but if the department says nothing, that probably means you are getting nothing.

When you receive your acceptance letter, you can make a good guess as to whether you are high or low on the totem pole. If three-fourths of the graduate students in a program are receiving some financial aid and you are offered none, you may have a hard time convincing the department that you should be supported in subsequent years. The offer that you get reflects the initial opinion the department has of you, and you have to do very well to change people's minds.

WILL THE MONEY KEEP COMING?

Will a fellowship or assistantship be renewed the following year? It's good news if a department offers you multiyear support, because many departments are reluctant to give firm guarantees. A three-year offer shows that you are one of the most sought-after students.

Many factors outside a department's control can affect the number of TA positions that will have to be filled at the last minute. It doesn't know if every student who has accepted an offer will show up, or even if one of last year's TAs will call to say that he has decided to find self-fulfillment in Nepal. People get sick, and TAs sometimes are offered late research assistantships when a professor gets a research grant. In that case their teaching job must be given to someone else.

On the other hand, a department may find in early April that more beginning students have accepted positions as TAs or fellows than it counted on. In that case, it may try to discourage late acceptances instead of making last-minute offers. But if you have an offer in writing, the university will honor it, no matter how overcommitted the department is. If it is overcommitted, you won't know it unless you hear some gossip in the halls after you arrive. The department will not send you a letter asking you to go somewhere else. Once you have an award, you will be on the same footing as all the other new graduate students with financial aid.

HOW MANY YEARS?

Since most departments do not know until the last minute the exact number of TAs they will be able to hire for an academic year, they don't like to give an absolute commitment that you will be reappointed. A typical situation is for you to be told that if your work is good, and if no financial crisis occurs in the department or the university, you can expect your assistantship to be renewed for several years. The number of years may be three, four, or five for a doctoral student, fewer for a master's student. The department wants to get you through to your degree as quickly as possible, and financial pressure is one way to encourage you to move fast. If you are promised financial aid, check to see if the department limits the number of years you can get it. If it takes you longer, you will have to support yourself with no help from the program. Ask what your chances are that the funding will be renewed.

You may be offered funds at the last minute. It's a great relief if you are, but it may mean that you will have to wait until the last minute to see whether your assistantship is renewed the following year. Some departments have a few overage graduate students who have been around forever, getting hired each year two days before school starts. They are usually very good teachers, but not very good students. They provide excellent teaching and cost the department very little because they are paid poorly. Don't become one of these people.

Many departments pay an experienced teaching assistant more than a beginner. If this is the case, your income may rise a little in the following years. You can ask about this, though it shouldn't be an important factor in deciding where to go.

Some departments use a highly questionable bait-and-switch tactic. They offer a good assistantship or fellowship for the first year or two and don't inform you that they routinely take away all support after the second year. Generally, the only way you can learn this is to ask the Graduate Adviser if this is what the department does, or talk to current graduate students. The department may not volunteer bad news, but it's unlikely that it will lie to you.

Does the department make a decision each year whether or not to renew your assistantship, or is it automatic if your work is good? Knowing this can make a big difference, as Chuck found out when he accepted an offer to work on his Ph.D. in sociology.

WHAT HAPPENED TO CHUCK, ROGER, AND ANDY

The first year Chuck was a teaching assistant, and when he was rehired for the second year he managed to support himself, his pregnant wife, and their baby son. But for the third year, his assistantship was taken away and given to a new student the department wanted to bring in.

Chuck managed to get a job as a library clerk, but he had to work quite a few hours a week; this meant he could not take as many courses each term and had to delay writing his dissertation. Chuck was in graduate school several years longer than he thought he would be, and when he finally got a position as an assistant professor he had a bigger debt to pay back than he had planned on.

Roger was accepted as a doctoral student in mathematics at a Big Ten university, but without any financial aid. He was told that he would very likely be appointed as a TA later, and since he was lucky enough to have his own money, he accepted. Two years later, even though Roger was a good student, he found that the department had changed its policy and was giving all its new TA appointments to entering students. Roger could get along without the money, but he was worried that without teaching experience he could never get the academic position he wanted. He protested that it wasn't fair to change the rules from what he had been told earlier, but it didn't do any good. He left and went to another Big Ten university that liked his record and needed TAs. He needed a year longer to get his degree because he had to take different courses after the transfer.

Sometimes, even if a department doesn't offer any financial aid, a student may decide it is worthwhile to choose that school.

When Andy graduated from Oberlin, he was admitted to the physics program with the offer of a good teaching assistantship at a big state university. He was also admitted to M.I.T., but with no money at all. After thinking it through, since he hoped to work at a research university, he decided it was worthwhile to him to go to M.I.T., which had a top reputation in physics, even if he had to take out student loans. He was hoping to do such good work at M.I.T. that after he had been there a while he would get an assistantship, but this didn't happen. He finished his degree with a big debt. He had hoped to be a college professor, but he ended up working in industrial research and earning more money.

GET THE OFFER IN WRITING

If you are offered any kind of financial aid by a member of the department in a conversation or telephone call, before you definitely decide to enroll in that program, be sure it is a firm commitment.

Katie was offered both a fellowship and a teaching job by the chairman of a department who was excited by her ideas about language and literature and wanted her to come and work on her Ph.D. with him. So that was where she chose to go, even though it would mean leaving California and its sunshine and beaches and living in cold northern Minnesota. But by the fall, when she moved there, she found out that the chairman had been hired away and gone to another university.

He had left nothing in writing about the fellowship and the teaching job, and his successor knew nothing about it. Katie managed to get a teaching assistant-ship, but she ended up with much less money. Sadder and wiser, she advises all potential graduate students who are offered financial aid: "Get it in writing. Be sure you have a firm commitment which is spelled out."

VISIT THE DEPARTMENTS

If you are still undecided, try to visit the schools before you make the final choice. We talked about visiting in Chapter 3, but now you have an offer. Things look different when you are on the verge of a decision. Even if you have visited before, now that you are admitted a second visit will help you decide. You will probably be treated differently, since the program has decided it wants you. Call the department's Graduate Adviser and ask if you can have appointments to meet some of the faculty who teach in the areas that interest you.

When you get there, go see them. Are the professors accessible? Will they talk to you and keep appointments? Do they seem interested?

It is difficult to find out how well their graduate students do when they finish. You can ask the Graduate Adviser, who may or may not be helpful. Or you might have to rely on gossip from students.

Try to see anyone you hope to work with, and find out if he or she welcomes students, and will be on campus when you arrive. Does this professor help graduate students to get their degrees? Or is this a person interested only in his or her own career? Does the professor keep making one demand after another so that the students spend years and some never finish?

This is a crucial point, as Lynn found out after she had been working on her Ph.D. in English for years; whenever she was close to finishing, her adviser wanted her to do something more. She took a job at the university press when her time as a TA ran out. As she got more interested in the press job, she kept saying, with less and less conviction, that she was working on her thesis. Finally she made the decision to forget the degree and go for a career in editing and publishing. She's not unhappy, but she wasted years.

This is something that you must prevent from happening. Talk to as many graduate students as you can. If the professor in the field you are interested in has had several students who have not finished, avoid him, and if he is the only one in that area, think long and hard before choosing to go to that school.

Try to find faculty members at the school who will tell you honestly what your chances are of getting the kind of job the program prepares you for, and how long it usually takes students to get the degree.

A good source of job information is current students or those who have recently received their degrees. They can tell you which graduates did get good jobs and which did not. The Graduate Adviser may have some statistics on what happened to recent graduates, but some graduates don't bother to tell their old departments what they do after they leave.

You will probably be introduced to some graduate students. But tell the Graduate Adviser that you want to look around by yourself. That way you can talk to other students. To find them, prowl the halls looking for offices that have many names on the door. Just walk in and introduce yourself as a person who might want to study there. Graduate students may give you an earful, and you have to evaluate what they say. You may have found only the discontented ones. Don't be discouraged if you are brushed off; universities have their share of rude people. If you look, you will find other people who will talk to you. They will be more interested in you because you are trying to make up your mind, and will probably encourage you or discourage you strongly.

KEEP TALKING TO PEOPLE

Walk through the building. Look around for yourself. Does it seem to be a pleasant and interesting place? You don't want to go to a department that has financial worries and is fearful that it may be downsized. Do you feel comfortable, and would you like to work here with these faculty and students? Explore the campus. Read the flyers on the bulletin boards. What about the library? The computer facilities?

Walk around the town. What about housing? Shopping? Will this town be a place where you can live and be happy?

Even after you have studied the official information the university sends you, continue to talk to people who know the program. A woman should talk to other female students to see what they say about the treatment they are getting there, particularly in some scientific and technical fields, which up to now have been dominated by men.

And last of all, look at the newspapers and see how expensive it will be to live in this town. The want ads for rentals will tell you quite a bit. Different places have wildly different costs of living. The salary for an assistantship that would be more than adequate in Columbia, Missouri, might not go far in San Francisco or New York.

STILL CAN'T DECIDE? THEN BARGAIN!

If you still can't make up your mind between two or more schools, you are in a good position. It's much better to have two offers than one or none. You can then talk to the Graduate Advisers to see if they are able to raise the offer. Of your two offers, one probably is for more money, while you really prefer the other. After all, if one of the schools has a better department and also offers the most financial aid, you shouldn't be undecided.

Talk to the Graduate Adviser at the place where the financial aid is low. Explain your situation truthfully, and ask whether there is any possibility that the amount could be increased. The Graduate Adviser may be able to raise the financial aid on the spot, or may have to consult others, or may say no, but you haven't lost anything. The Graduate Adviser now knows that you are a sought-after student, and that may help your reputation a bit.

CHECKLIST

Finally, if you are not completely certain, take a pencil and paper, make parallel columns and write down the pros and cons of each department you are thinking about. Here are some of the things to consider:

- What is the reputation of the program?
- Will you be able to work in areas that interest you?
- How accessible is the faculty?
- What are your chances of working with the professor you want?
- If you are promised financial aid, for how long will you get it? Can it be renewed?
- What about tuition and fees?
- Average number of years until degree?
- What about jobs for graduates?
- Do you feel comfortable with the faculty and students?
- What about university facilities:
    the library?
    computers?
    offices, laboratory, or studio?
- What do current graduate students say about:
    the program?
    the faculty?
    jobs for recent graduates?
    student morale?
- Do you like the city and the setting of the university?
- Cost of living?
- Housing?
- Proximity to your family? (This can be a plus or a minus, depending on your family.)

10

IF YOU ARE
NOT ADMITTED

> *It was one of the worst days of my life. At first I was angry. Then I got depressed and wondered if there was any point at all in trying to go to graduate school or if I should just give up and stay in the same dumb job until I was old enough to retire. Why did I ever think I could do it? Two days later when I woke up, I was still angry, but this time I did something about it. Those jerks who had turned me down were wrong. I didn't know how, but I made up my mind that I would start again.*
>
> —*MARGARET*

WHAT IF YOU do not get into the program you hoped for? At worst it's a delay, a detour, not a dead end, and does not mean you are not good enough for graduate-level education. This is an opportunity to grow and prepare for next year's application process. And now you know much more about the different hurdles you have to overcome—the tests, the references, the essay, and so on—and can make them all better.

You may not have been admitted for any number of reasons. The department's budget may have been cut so that it couldn't admit all the people it had anticipated, or it may have had a big number of exceptionally qualified students competing for a limited number of places. The professors on the committee may have different interests from yours, or they may have made the wrong decision and rejected students who would do very well in that program. A string of chance events that you could not possibly anticipate, and which were out of your control, may have relegated your application to the bottom of the pile. These things happen. Don't assume you have glaring, unfixable faults that kept you out.

You might be able to ask the Graduate Adviser why you were turned down. Write a polite letter or make a telephone call, but be sure to keep your cool. He or she may be able to give you an idea; possibly not, since all decisions have been made by committees. Most likely you will get an equally polite rejoinder saying that they had many well-qualified applicants and that they were unable to admit all those who could have succeeded. However, it's possible that you will get some encouraging information.

WHAT NEXT?

So, what can you do about the situation? You know that your application materials were not judged to be in the top group at the places where you applied. You should review these carefully and see whether you can improve them in any way. If you are still determined, you can try some different courses of action. One is to do what Herb did, which was to ask for admission as a non-degree student.

When he was refused admittance as a Ph.D. student in linguistics at a Big Ten university, Herb went to see the Graduate Adviser and told him that he knew that his undergraduate grades were not good enough, but he had grown up since college and was now a serious student. And, he said, he knew linguistics was something he wanted to spend his life doing and was sure he could make contributions to the field. Would they give him a chance to prove it?

The department still would not let him enter as a Ph.D. candidate, but agreed to admit him as a non-degree student. That would enable him to take graduate courses but would not commit the department. If he really could do it, if he got good grades and good recommendations from the professors who taught the courses, he might be able to persuade people to change their minds.

Herb decided to spend a year as a non-degree student and take graduate courses, to see if he could do the work. It might have been wasted time, but then if he had not been able to, he would have learned that he was not cut out to work in linguistics.

But he did it. He worked harder than he ever had and impressed two of the linguistics professors, who gave him glowing recommendations after the first semester. He was admitted, and the following year had a teaching assistantship.

A GAMBLE

What Herb did was a big gamble. But he figured since linguistics was what he wanted to do, he would take the chance. In fact, he was not gambling a whole year, just the first semester. The admissions decisions are made in the middle of the second semester, so he had only his work in the first semester to convince the department to change its decision.

If, at the end of the first semester, he had been unable to get good recommendations, or if his enthusiasm had waned, he would have left immediately. As it was, with his good grades and the recommendations his instructors wrote, he decided to continue as a non-degree student the second semester, and didn't find out until April that he had been successful and was admitted for the fall. After he enrolled, he petitioned to have the graduate courses he had taken while he'd been a non-degree student count toward his Ph.D. His petition was granted.

Other people who can't afford to become full-time students can take extension courses that meet on the weekends or evenings and use good grades in those to get into a program.

Phyllis was working five days a week in Dallas while she took Saturday morning classes. When her extension instructors saw how hard she worked, they realized that she was a serious, committed student, and were glad to recommend her for graduate school.

YOU CAN APPLY TO BE A MASTER'S STUDENT

If you are rejected for a doctoral program, you can reapply to be admitted as a master's candidate. Admission requirements for the master's degree are usually not as rigorous as for Ph.D. students. If you do well in the master's program, you will improve your chances of being admitted later as a doctoral candidate. And if your work does not distinguish you as a brilliant researcher, you will finish up with a master's degree and reap the benefits that will bring, such as a higher salary.

YOU CAN TAKE THE GRE AGAIN AND REWRITE YOUR ESSAY

You can't do anything about your undergraduate grades, but by yourself you can improve two parts of your application, your test scores and your essay, and work on a third—the letters of recommendation.

You can take the GRE or the test for your profession again. You will probably do better, since you now know the format, and you will be able to prepare more thoroughly. Most programs will look at your most recent tests scores and discount the earlier ones. You might want to take a course in preparing for the test. Sometimes students can make striking improvements. Really good GRE or professional test scores can overcome some mediocre grades you might have earned as an undergraduate.

Look again at your essay. The essay is something that many graduate students say is the hardest thing to do. They don't know what the faculty wants or what they should say. It's hard to judge what you have written by yourself; you are too close to it. Try to get some knowledgeable person to criticize it. Do you come across as highly competent and enthusiastic, but not arrogant? An outside review by a reliable person can be valuable. Read Chapter 6 again.

You can also ask for recommendations from different people (see Chapter 7). You may have had the feeling that one of your recommenders was not eager to write that letter. Even though you tried to get the best letters you could, you might have made a mistake in your choice of letter writers. One lackluster letter can make a bad impression. You are working in the dark here, because you cannot read the letters, but you may have an uncertain feeling about one of your recommenders. If you can, replace that letter with another.

TRY DIFFERENT SCHOOLS, OR REAPPLY TO SOME

Finally, you can apply to different programs for the following year. There are probably quite a few programs that you could have applied to. You can choose universities at the same level, but in slightly less desirable locations. You can lower your sights a bit and apply to slightly less prestigious departments. You know quite a lot about the various options now, and it shouldn't take too long to choose different places to apply to.

You can also reapply to the same places that rejected you before, but it's sometimes difficult to change committee members' minds. They will have kept your application from the previous year, possibly with notes or comments from various faculty members. In order to get a fresh evaluation, give the committee some new evidence. If you have been taking courses, or if you have been working at a professional job in the field, emphasize that in a cover letter. Tell how you have changed and now are a better prospect than you were before. Present yourself in a fresh light, so they do not just recycle their old evaluation. But, on the whole, it's better to try different programs.

Rejection is a setback, but you can recover from it. Keep your belief in yourself, and don't let negative evaluations by unknown committees shake your confidence. If you really want to get that graduate degree, you can do it. And now you know a lot about applying; the whole process will be a great deal easier than it was the first time around.

PART 3 YOU ARE IN

CHAPTER 11

A GOOD START

> *I did it. I got admitted to the graduate program that was my first choice, and with an assistantship, too. At first I was ecstatic. Then I began to wonder what it would be like. I had never been a graduate student before. I would be going to classes with those confident students, all of whom would know their way around. I was a little frightened, but determined to learn all I could and to do well. And I did.*
>
> —*MARY ELLEN*

YOU'VE MADE IT! And soon you will be starting graduate school.

You are going to make a complete change in your life, and once you take this step, there is no going back. You've been thinking about this for a long time, but check the reality of the situation against what you expected when you started the process.

Look at the costs; this is crucial. You will have to live and pay tuition and other expenses on your income, loans, and savings. Most financial aid offices provide an estimated budget for student expenses. That is a good place to start. If your offer contains financial aid, look it over again. It should specify in writing how much you will receive, and you should be able to estimate pretty closely what you will get after deductions. Before you get started, review the finances so you will not have any unpleasant surprises. Make a rough budget so you know how much you will be able to spend on housing. Maybe you can live without a car, and spend more on an apartment close to campus. Review the alternatives, so you can make reasonable decisions when you get there.

A NEW LIFE

All right, you have thought it over and are planning to begin your new life. Let's suppose you are starting in the fall.

First, you will need a place to live. Visit your new locality as soon as possible, months before the term starts if you can, to find housing. Other students arrive in town well before the new semester to rent apartments and rooms; as the summer goes on, there will be fewer choices. In a large city the ebb and flow of students does not make much difference, but in many university towns housing is scarce in the fall. There may be a university office that helps students find housing. The Dean of Students Office will at least know where to find it. Most university neighborhoods have a lot of student housing, often including graduate student dormitories. With luck, your housing search shouldn't take long.

While you are there, drop in to see the Graduate Adviser to discuss your program. The GA will be very busy at the beginning of the fall term but will be glad to talk to you at this quiet, less chaotic time. He or she will be looking at you in a new light. Before you were an applicant; now you are a new student and possibly a TA or a fellow—you are a junior colleague.

The GA wants to get to know you and wants you to succeed, and you want to make a good impression. He or she probably had a lot to do with selecting you, and wants you to get as good a start as possible. The department's reputation depends partly on the students it turns out, and now you are one of them.

Before your conversation, have in mind the requirements of the program. You can discuss courses you might take, and the way your undergraduate work has prepared you for this program, and where you hope the program will lead. Be prepared to have something to say. The GA is the overall academic supervisor and has a strong influence on who gets teaching assistantships and other appointments. If you can't remember the courses you have taken or the names of the topics covered, it will seem that you don't have any real interest in your field. If you are going to be teaching, remember that you are probably talking to an old pro.

First appearances are important, and how you look will have some influence on how seriously you are taken. If you are starting medical school, don't make your first visit in a tie-dyed T-shirt and torn jeans. No one wants to go to a doctor who does not look clean. If you are going into an M.B.A. program, at the initial interview it is a good idea to look like a grown-up who will be working in the business world. However, applicants in liberal arts and many other programs have great freedom to express themselves in their clothes.

THE ACADEMIC YEAR BEGINS

At the beginning of the year the university will almost certainly have an orientation program for new graduate students which will help you get started. Your department will have an additional orientation session, too.

There are two main aspects to this orientation. First, if you are going to be teaching, or doing other work for the department, your duties will be described. Second, as a student you will have to plan your academic program.

If you have a paid position in the department, your job will be carefully explained, particularly if you will be teaching. You may be involved in practice sessions in which each student has to give a ten-minute explanation of some topic to a group of fellow students and one or two faculty members. Whether you are assigned to teach or just to be a grader may depend on how well you do in this practice session.

This part of the orientation is the responsibility of a departmental administrator such as the Associate Head. He or she is very concerned that the term gets off to a smooth start, and your preparation should be good. But if there is anything you don't understand, be sure to get it cleared up. You don't want to be the monkey wrench in the machinery on the first day.

You will probably also have a faculty adviser, who may or may not continue to be your adviser throughout the program. When the term starts, there is a lot of confusion; everyone is busy, and the faculty members who are organizing the year's work are under great pressure. It will help them, and you, if you have planned what you want to do and ask questions that you have thought through. Before you talk to your adviser, try to plan the courses you are going to take in the first term. As you do, you will automatically find things that you need to ask about.

There is great variation in the quality of advice you may get. Some professors like to talk to students and know all about the different options available, including the courses and their prerequisites, and the requirements of different departmental programs. Others may be remote, not well up on requirements for students, and may give only perfunctory advice. If you get such an adviser, try to change advisers at the first opportunity. If you can't get an official change, try during your first semester to develop an informal relationship with a more agreeable faculty member.

Your first adviser may not have much more information about you than your name. If there is a folder about you, he or she probably won't have looked at it very carefully. At your first meeting, describe your present educational status clearly, and say what you want to accomplish. Try to get a clear idea of the sequence of courses and examinations that are required in your program. If you are a master's student, you may be able to rough out a schedule for most of the required work very early.

It's important to choose your initial courses carefully. The courses in your new program may not mesh very well with the work you did before. Most classes have prerequisites, but they are usually given as specific courses at your new university. The only way to figure out what you can handle is to compare the prerequisite courses listed with what you have already studied. A good adviser can be invaluable, but you must be able to describe the courses you took and the topics they covered. Your adviser should then be able to tell you where you will fit into the program.

What you want to know is: Given my situation and my goals, what courses should I take, and in what order? Later you will need to learn about preparing for general examinations, but you want to leave this first interview with, at least, a list of your classes for the first term. Even doing this can be tricky. If some course that you want is only offered rarely, it might be better to take it now and delay some required course that is taught every year.

What about getting graduate credit for courses taken elsewhere? You may have taken a graduate course or two as an undergraduate, in addition to the requirements for your bachelor's degree. You should check to see whether you can receive credit for them toward a graduate degree at your new university. If so, you will probably have to make a petition with a full description of the courses, and go through a certain amount of red tape. But if you are working on a master's degree, the credit you receive could shorten the time needed by a semester. If this is a possibility, don't take a class that substantially overlaps one that you took elsewhere, for then you won't get any transfer credit.

Also talk to graduate students who are already in your program. But bear in mind that a lot of misinformation may be floating around, so try to verify information that sounds strange. Many faculty members are also not clear on prerequisites, rules, and requirements.

NO FINANCIAL AID?

If you are admitted to an academic program without financial aid and want to enroll, you will have to decide very soon whether you will stop with a master's or continue on for the doctorate.

You should try to be awarded an assistantship for the second year. Even if you don't need the money, an assistantship will show that you are a first-rate student, and will give you many more contacts in the department. If the department evaluated you when you first applied and offered no support, you will have to do superbly in your first semester to get the faculty to change their minds. The first semester is vital, because basic TA hiring decisions are made before the results of the second semester are in. Also, your department may be looking for TAs at the last minute, and, if they are, you want them to think of you.

The first-year requirements for the master's and the doctoral degrees may differ, and if they do you will have to choose one track or the other. Of course, a master's degree is not going to take as much time, and you do not have to plan for seven years of financial pain. Even getting through two years with no support from the program is formidable, but many students manage to do it, often with the help of loans. In some fields, such as computer science, an M.S. will make you more employable, so it is worth it. But if you are interested in a Ph.D. in history, and are admitted without financial aid, you will have to think long and hard about what you want to do.

Master's students generally have a fairly definite program to follow, with required courses and possibly a general examination or an expository thesis. It may be possible to get a master's degree without putting much effort into it or attracting any attention, particularly if there is no thesis requirement. You will then get an undistinguished degree, and when you finish, it may get you a better job.

But when you finish, if you haven't put much into it, you will have missed the intellectual excitement of graduate school; the degree will be merely an addition to your bachelor's degree, another qualification. If you are a master's student, get as involved as possible. Your time as a student will be more rewarding.

OFF TO A GOOD START

From the first day of classes, do your best work, and talk to the instructors. Choose subjects that you enjoy, taught by approachable professors. It helps if you have been in town a few days and have talked to advanced graduate students. They can give you uncensored opinions about the faculty. Most faculty members will get mixed reviews, but you should try hard to avoid any professor who is universally panned.

If you are interested in the courses, you will have comments and questions about the material. You want the professors to know you. Your standing in the department depends not so much on your grades as on the faculty members' impressions of you.

Most departments are small societies; faculty members know each other well, and talk about the graduate students. You should try to do an outstanding job in one or two of your courses, rather than just to do pretty well in all of them. Of course, this doesn't mean you should neglect any class. If you don't keep all your grades up, you won't remain in graduate school for long. Still, choose one or two courses for your best work. If you are outstanding in a course, the professor will notice you and talk about your work.

Not every professor wants to talk to students; some of them are remote personalities whose interest is primarily in their research. See how your professors interact with students.

If you are a teaching assistant, you have an advantage. You will be supervised by at least one faculty member, and will be able to talk to other TAs and to professors about any problems that arise in teaching, and how to deal with them. You will have more contact with the professors and can learn what is happening in the department.

GET TO KNOW THE FACULTY

Whether or not you are teaching, you should get acquainted with the faculty. Some of them will want to talk to you, so talk to them. Now that you have been admitted, they want you to succeed.

Most departments have seminars, colloquia, or special lectures that any student or faculty member can attend. As a beginning student, you may find that you don't really understand what is being said, but you should go to some of them and keep trying. For one thing, it will introduce you to different areas of your field, and to faculty members and the research they are doing.

These lectures are often preceded or followed by a coffee hour or some social occasion. You may feel awkward speaking with a faculty member, but people usually like to talk about their work, and with any luck you'll be curious about their work and ideas in your field. Faculty members feel that their specialty is an important area; they enjoy talking to and working with students who are eager to learn and who show that they will be good at it. After a while you will find that it is easier to talk to them. But if you don't speak to the faculty and nobody knows who you are, later on it will be much more difficult for you to get good recommendations.

There is another plus about the department receptions, says Susan, who remembers how little money she had during the years she was in graduate school. At these teas or coffee hours, poverty-stricken graduate students can stock up on food. "We quickly learned that you were often offered something to eat," she says. "It was a great way to supplement our meager rations."

FINDING OUT REQUIREMENTS

If you are in a professional program, you know just how many years will elapse before you finish law school or medical school or get the M.B.A. Usually the requirements are thoroughly spelled out.

But in graduate school there will be requirements that are not printed in the catalog. One annoying task is finding out exactly what they are.

You need to know the exact sequence of examinations you will have to pass, and should try to get a clear idea of the material they cover and the times when they are given. You may be able to take specific courses that prepare you for these examinations, but there is a basic conflict between students and faculty. Students always want to know exactly what material will be covered, while teachers don't want to be tied to a rigid syllabus. Also, on the way to your degree, you may have to pass the various hurdles by specific times.

The department will provide, in some written form, a list of requirements and examinations for each of its programs. You should also be able to get a schedule of deadlines for passing certain exams or course work. The Graduate Adviser is responsible for keeping this information complete and current, but it still may not contain everything you need to know.

One thing that changes from year to year is the calendar. In each term there will be last dates to add or drop a course, and last dates to submit a thesis or take a thesis examination. Such information is not hard to find, but you have to know that it exists.

The Graduate College of your university may have additional rules, for example, requirements for the number of semesters you must be in residence for a given degree. It is also common for it to have fairly elaborate rules about the format of any thesis you have to submit. This submission is the final step in thesis approval, after your departmental faculty committee has passed on it.

When Marco submitted his Ph.D. thesis in anthropology, the dragon lady in the Graduate College who scanned each thesis for any typos or errors found out that there was no page 11 in his thesis. The thesis made sense, but somehow the page numbering was wrong. Marco did not want to reprint the whole thesis, so before returning it to the Graduate College he added a page 11 that fitted in linguistically but made no sense anthropologically. No one who understood anthropology ever saw the new page 11. The only one who did was the functionary in the Graduate College. After it passed the Graduate College format person and was deposited in the library, Marco took a razor blade and removed the offending page.

It is not likely that Graduate College regulations will impede you, but it's good to know that there are such things, probably buried deep in their printed general rules.

Some time during your first term, you should try to make up a tentative schedule of courses, examinations, and thesis requirements. If you are a master's student, this schedule might be fairly complete, but a beginning doctoral student can't make a definite plan that will cover more than a couple of years. It's too early to choose a research area and a thesis adviser, since your interests may change as you progress. You should go over this plan with your adviser. If you don't have confidence in your adviser, make an appointment with the Graduate Adviser. You can find out if there are any serious omissions in your list of things to do.

For a professional degree or a master's program such as the M.S.W. in social work or the M.Arch. program, you should take as many of the required courses as possible during the first year and establish yourself as a first-rate student. Learn what you are responsible for, and map out your program as far ahead as you can. When you have finished your required courses, you will probably have some electives, and in these you can try to do an outstanding job.

One thing is fairly certain; you won't be able to make a plan that works without changes. A professor who teaches a certain course may go on sabbatical leave, or leave permanently. A course may be canceled if not enough students register. Developments in the field may result in a new course that you really should take. Still, do your best to plan ahead, and also keep an eye on the real world that is waiting for you. For example, a course in computer-aided design may not be required in an architecture program, but it is almost essential to have one in order to get hired as a beginning architect.

As you progress, you can try to take charge of your program as much as possible. Occasionally the Graduate Adviser will waive a course that, strictly speaking, you should take, or let you make a substitution. You may be able to avoid a course with a bad reputation. If you do this, get permission in writing to avert trouble later. Of course, most requirements are fixed in stone, but don't be afraid to try to tailor the program to your interests. You may get a lot more out of your degree.

REFERENCES ARE CRUCIAL

Whether you are a master's degree student who needs a job, or a doctoral student who wants a fellowship or an assistantship, recommendations from within the department are critical. When the time comes to make awards, a strong recommendation from one faculty member carries a lot of weight. And later on, if a professor happens to find out about a job opening, you want your name to be the one that comes to mind.

If you don't single yourself out in any way, even if you do good work and get A grades, you will be at a disadvantage when you need references. Faculty members will write letters saying that, yes, you are an excellent student, but they won't be able to say much more. The faculty have to know you and think well of you. If they can make specific comments on your enthusiasm, your attendance at seminars in your area, the excellence of a particular paper you wrote, or your stimulating participation in class, the letter will be much more effective.

Your accomplishments before you became a student no longer matter. What you are doing now is what counts.

DOCTORAL PROGRAMS

The average doctoral student devotes between five and ten years to earning the degree, much longer than the master's student, and the requirements are more complicated.

Ph.D. programs vary, but there are usually two comprehensive examinations. One of them will test your knowledge over broad areas in your field. The other is usually narrower and deeper and covers the area in which you will write your dissertation.

The first general examination may be called a Qualifying Examination, or can have some other title such as Comprehensive Examination. It covers the basic areas in your field of study, and is based loosely on courses that you take to prepare yourself. Its usual purpose is to see whether you are qualified to go beyond the master's toward a Ph.D. Some programs have a formal structure in which a student is admitted to the Ph.D. program only after passing this hurdle. There can be a set of rules for how many times you can attempt this exam, and whether you can pass it in stages or must do it all at once. You also may be required to pass it within a certain number of terms.

It is often administered by a committee of faculty members, who prepare and grade the exam. The membership of this committee will change from year to year, so the exam may vary in content and difficulty. An effort is made to keep the exams fair and uniform, but it's difficult to do this with so many personalities involved. However, the committee members are all scholars and researchers in the field, and will prepare an exam that they think is reasonable.

This exam will usually cover several basic areas in your field, and will be given in parts. If it is a written exam, you may have to produce a two- or three-hour examination paper per day for several days. If it is oral, the individual sessions rarely last more than an hour, and the whole thing may be over in one day. Oral examinations are more stressful for some people, but they are mercifully short. Students generally prefer written exams because of this stress factor, but the percentage of students who pass oral exams is about the same as for written exams. This qualifying exam is usually the most difficult one in your life as a graduate student. In fact, it may be the most difficult examination in your entire life.

The second general examination is often called the Preliminary Examination. It's the last major exam you take before writing your thesis. It's "preliminary" to writing the thesis, but by the time you take it you are a fairly accomplished scholar, ready to start research in your field. In most programs this second examination is easier to pass than the first one. It usually covers your area of expertise. You will probably have a thesis adviser by the time you take it, and your adviser won't let you go ahead unless you are ready for it. Usually an oral examination, it's given by a committee of faculty members who are experts in your area within the field. While it's not exactly easy, it's much rarer for a student to fail the second exam than the first.

These exam descriptions are meant to be generic. There is a lot of variation in the names, formats, level of difficulty, and rules from one program to another. But it is almost always true that one general examination tests your knowledge of the field as a whole, and another focuses on your area of research.

After your years of classes, you finish the degree by writing your dissertation, or thesis, which is a substantial piece of original work in your particular area. The last hurdle is the Final Examination, or Thesis Defense. This is always an oral examination on your thesis research before an expert faculty committee, including your adviser. It is very rare to fail this exam, though students usually are required to make revisions in the dissertation. After all, your adviser has certified that you are ready to take the exam. Only if something is terribly wrong with the thesis will you fail.

WHAT THE EXAMS COVER

One thing that bothers students is that faculty are often vague about what the qualifying exams will cover, and often there are no courses that specifically prepare students for the examination. If the topic is "Nineteenth-Century American Literature" or "Differential Geometry," there is more to know than anyone can possibly learn. The faculty ask questions that they feel are reasonable, but they don't want to spell out in advance exactly what will be included. They may think that you should know what the most important topics are, without having them laid out in detail. Still, try to get a clear idea of what you should know for these examinations. Talk to different faculty members. Ask other students who have passed it.

Your department may have old examinations on file. If it does, get copies. But remember that, like much work in the academic world, the exam was probably written by a committee. The committee for your exam may produce something completely different from the exams on file.

WHAT ABOUT THE LANGUAGE TEST?

For some doctorates you are required to be able to read material in your field in one or two foreign languages, with the aid of a dictionary. The language may be specified, or you may have some choice. This is not a very difficult requirement, and many universities offer special language classes for graduate students. Others allow graduate students to take undergraduate courses, and some will accept good grades in these courses in lieu of the language examinations. You don't have to speak or write the language, and many students with a couple of semesters of undergraduate German, say, can pass the exam with a little preparation.

It's very easy to put off the language requirement, but the time will come when, if you haven't done it, you won't be making "satisfactory progress." This situation can easily jeopardize your financial aid, and may cause other trouble. Plan to get these requirements out of the way as soon as possible.

BARRY'S MISTAKE

Don't let the deadlines take you by surprise.

Barry enjoyed reading Latin American literature and liked teaching Spanish to freshman students but didn't want to think about taking the examinations. He put the exams and the other requirements out of mind. In January, early in his fourth semester, he found a note in his mailbox from the Graduate Adviser telling him to come to the office. There he was told that unless he passed the Comprehensive Examination in March, the next time it was given, he would have no assistantship for the following year.

Meager as his assistant's salary was, it was what had kept Barry alive. Without it, he would have to leave school. He suddenly saw how important the faculty felt it was for students to progress according to schedule. Each spring semester a committee decided which second-year students to reappoint to teaching assistantships. Before they would offer a third year, they required every student to pass the Comprehensive Examination.

Until then, Barry hadn't realized how seriously they would take this requirement. But he worked night and day for the next two months, lost five pounds, and passed the Comprehensive Exam.

THE TIMING OF REAPPOINTMENTS

Before the end of the spring term, departments have to decide which students to reappoint for the next academic year. If you are a beginning student, they will have to decide about your second-year appointment on the basis of only your first semester's work.

The same thing happens a year later. They will probably decide who is to get an assistantship for the third year on the basis of three semesters of work. Even if you do brilliantly in your fourth semester, it will probably be too late to influence the department to give you financial aid for your third year.

There may be a departmental schedule that describes "satisfactory progress toward a degree," which says that you must pass various exams and satisfy requirements by certain times in your second, third, or fourth years. In these cases, the timing will usually be set so the department can use the exam results in deciding on appointments and fellowships for the following year. Find the schedule and pay close attention to its deadlines.

GRADUATE STUDENT ASSOCIATIONS

If the department has a graduate student association, check it out. Some are very helpful; others are a big waste of time. At the very least, it is a way to make friends and a place to learn about some of the faculty members' quirks and interests. You will have plenty of opportunity to talk to fellow students about how things are done in the department, but they should be students who have been around a while. Be skeptical, though; remember that a lot of misinformation may be going around.

Some students spend a lot of time on these associations, or on a graduate assistants' union. These are worthy things to do, but they can take up a lot of time. Some people really enjoy this kind of work; unless you are one of them, don't get deeply involved right away. These organizations have no bearing on your progress toward a degree.

DEPARTMENTAL GOVERNANCE

Academic departments vary a lot in how they are run, but there are two main types. One of them is a department with a Head and an Advisory Committee, in which the Head has quite a lot of power. The other is a department with a Chair and an Executive Committee. Here the Chair has a lot of influence, but the Executive Committee has the last word. Still, the general style of governance is what is called "collegial," with a lot of input from colleagues, either informally or formally through committees.

Most departments have numerous committees, which either decide or give advice on the activities of the department. The most important committees are those dealing with promotions and awards of tenure, with salary increases, and with decisions on hiring. These committees are not likely to have graduate student members. But with many other committees, the input of graduate students may be sought, though an entering student will probably not be appointed to one of them. These include, for example, the scheduling of graduate courses, orientation of new graduate students, handling formal complaints about teaching, and deciding on teaching awards both for faculty and graduate assistants. Any issue that concerns the graduate students and that does not affect the core functions of the department may have formal graduate student input; it's possible for graduate students to make a real contribution.

Committee work takes time, but it does have some advantages. Aside from the opportunity to have some influence, you will get a better idea of how the department works. When the time comes, being on an important committee will provide a line or two on your resumé. It shows that you took some interest in your department, and that people thought well enough of you to ask for your input. Again, be careful not to overdo it—committees can soak up a lot of time.

SUPERVISORS

If you have a research assistantship, your supervisor will be the professor you are working for. If you are teaching, your teaching boss may be an Associate Head of the department. This faculty member decides who will teach what course, arranges the teaching schedules, and handles all complaints about teaching. The Graduate Adviser is the one who follows your academic progress.

Ordinarily you will have contact with the Graduate Adviser only when something good or bad happens. You may be notified that you have been awarded fellowship funds, or that your assistantship is in danger of not being extended. The GA usually keeps track of the academic progress of every graduate student in the program.

Your original application papers, grade records, progress in passing language and general examination requirements, letters of recommendation, committee assignments—in fact, the elements making up the whole paper trail of your life in graduate school—are in the Graduate Adviser's office. A summary is probably kept in a computerized database. When the time comes to make TA appointments or to award fellowship funds, these records, together with recommendations from the faculty, form the basis for those decisions.

If problems arise, some students are reluctant to bring them to the Graduate Adviser because that office may be the one that makes reappointments and has a lot to do with awarding fellowships. They are afraid that if they reveal their troubles, it will be held against them. But most Graduate Advisers will do what they can to help, and if you have a serious problem your supervisors are going to find out about it sooner or later anyway.

DON'T LET A MINOR MISTAKE HURT YOU

Do what is supposed to be done. Meet all the deadlines in your work; for example, don't slack off so much that you have to ask a teacher to give you a deferred grade, to be made up by finishing the work later. If you have an assistantship, do the work faithfully and on time. Besides affecting your reputation in the department and your chances of good recommendations when you need them, if you don't do what you are supposed to when you are supposed to, it hurts other people. Your own students and your colleagues are depending on you. Sometimes, minor mistakes can really hurt.

Suppose you are teaching one section of a big course, and you forget a joint grading session with the other TAs and the professor. First they wait for you, then they try to call, and finally they do your share of the work, too. Your name is mud for a long time.

If you have a problem that you can't solve by yourself, the Graduate Adviser can help. You are not expected to be able to handle everything. For example, you probably have been assigned an academic adviser to discuss the courses you should take. Maybe it's impossible to find this person, or maybe you can't get any sensible advice. Go to see the Graduate Adviser. This will not be the first time the problem has occurred, perhaps with the same faculty member as the culprit.

If the Graduate Adviser cannot help to solve the problem, he or she can put you in touch with some office or individual who can. The adviser is not there just to keep track of your work and to make decisions, but to help you through and to try to make the graduate program as good as it can possibly be.

BECOMING A TEACHER

Many graduate students who get financial aid receive it for being teaching assistants. Being a teaching assistant requires a brand-new skill—teaching.

Teaching college students is a whole new world. Getting up and facing your first class is frightening. Fortunately, teaching your first class happens only one time.

If you are a teaching assistant, you will probably spend several hours a week in front of a class. As a beginning graduate student, usually you will not be given total responsibility for a course, but will work under supervision. Often the professor in charge lectures to all the students, who are then divided into sections for discussions, problem solving, laboratory work, or something similar. You might be in charge of one or more of these smaller sections, and be expected to do whatever the professor tells you to do. For these classes you will have to prepare thoroughly and also be available to the students for a certain number of office hours each week.

RESPONSIBILITY AND WORK

Being a teaching assistant is a responsible position, and can involve a lot of work. At first you may have trouble managing your time. One issue to resolve is how much time to spend on your teaching.

Do a good job with your teaching, but remember that what is most important to the faculty is your work as a student, not as a teacher. During your first year you should concentrate on academic work. Don't slack off on teaching, but don't let it take over your life.

Bruce Reznick, in his booklet *Chalking It Up: Advice to a New TA*, cites two extreme types of new teaching assistants. One of them devotes so much of his attention to his teaching that he neglects his own studies; he "gives students his home phone number as a 24-hour hot line for student problems. He gives two extra review sessions before each test and encourages students to ask for make-up exams if they are just not ready."

But unless teaching assistants give their own work priority and stay afloat, they will not be TAs next year.

Neither will the other extreme type of TA that Reznick cites, who does not bother to prepare his lectures, cuts off questions in class, and is forever annoyed at the students, all of whom he lets know that he considers lazy and stupid.

When you are a TA, you are part of the public face of the university. Students will talk about you, and if you are not doing your job they may tell their parents. Department heads hate to get calls from parents saying that some sociology instructor is unfair, unprepared, or unintelligible. Don't attract this kind of attention.

That does not mean that you should overprepare. You should spend the first week of the term familiarizing yourself with the entire course. After that, two hours spent in preparation for each hour in class is usually sufficient. This may seem like a lot, but you can use some of your scheduled office hours to prepare, since students will not always be coming to see you. The next time you teach the course, you will need less time to get ready.

Going too fast or too slow is one of the biggest problems for a new teacher. Pacing yourself will become easier with experience. Many universities have an office called something like the Office of Instructional Resources that will help new teaching assistants. If you ask, a person from that office will make a videotape of you teaching. You can see how you appear to someone sitting in the class, and that office will discuss your teaching with you. Then if you have something to improve, you will be able to work on it. If you want to become a more effective teacher, ask in your department where you can go for help.

STARTING OFF

Now that you are a graduate student, go at it wholeheartedly. First impressions are important, and you are going to make a lot of them during your first year. You are entering a small society in which you and your work will be noticed. Academic life is different from "real life"; you leave a paper trail of course work, grades, and examination results. These records, as well as personal impressions, can help you in your future career. Study and keep your grades high, but remember that it's more important to seek mentors and, by your work in and out of class, win their confidence. If you make the most of your education, you can leave with good prospects, good recommendations, and a record to be proud of.

CHAPTER 12

MOVING AHEAD

> When I was an undergrad, I felt almost invisible in the big classrooms. I went to class because I wanted to learn and I needed good grades, but there were times I felt that if I did not go, no one would know or care. As soon as I started graduate school, many of the faculty talked to me and knew who I was. And right away I was part of a small group of other graduate students. Many of them became my good friends.
>
> —JACKIE

YOUR GOAL NOW is to stay in graduate school and to get that degree. But you really want more than the degree. You want to be in the top rank, a person who is known for good work and good ideas. Enthusiastic recommendations will give you a real edge in your career, and you want to show the faculty that you are one of the best.

You have settled down and are working hard on your courses. You know that you need to get mostly A's in order to be considered a promising student. Unlike college, in graduate school you can flunk out with a few C grades. B's are permitted but are not good.

You have planned ahead as much as possible, so that you won't be surprised by some requirement that you hadn't known about. Even so, some unforeseen situations may arise.

COMPETITION

If you come from a less demanding school, say a small liberal arts college, at first you may find graduate school course work overwhelming and the other students too competitive. Women, particularly in fields that have until recently been dominated by men, often feel this way.

The competing students probably aren't any brighter than you; it's just that they have been working harder, with tougher competition, for a long time. Remember, the admissions committee examined the applicants and judged that you were one who could do the work. Soon you will know the ropes and find that you can do much that seems difficult now.

Don't be psyched out by students who, when asked if they managed to solve a difficult problem, will reply dismissively, "There's nothing to it," not letting on that they stayed up working all night. These students are not necessarily the whizzes they would like to appear. Don't let them intimidate you. If the work is hard for you, most likely it is hard for them, too.

If you are worried that your preparation is not adequate for a course you are going to take, decide beforehand what you will do if it proves beyond you. It's a good idea to have a fallback plan. Suppose you want to take course B, and course A is a prerequisite although it is not actually required. When the term begins you can go to the professor who is teaching A and ask if you can sit in on the course. Say that you are signed up for B but are worried that you may not be ready for it; you might want to drop B and pick up A. Most faculty members will agree to this; they like to have students, and for advanced courses the class will not be too large. After just a few days of sitting in both A and B, you will know which one you should take.

TOO MUCH TO HANDLE?

But what do you do if the work continues to be too hard and you are not keeping up?

If a course is not going well, you will realize it very quickly, probably after just a few days in class. This is a difficult situation. Talk to the professor and see if there is extra work you can do to bring yourself up.

Perhaps you should drop the course and take a prerequisite

course first. Instead of a too-difficult class, switch to one that is at a lower level that will give you the background you need.

It's easy to convince yourself that things will get better, the mist will clear from your brain, and you will start to forge ahead in the difficult class. However, this does not often happen. Give yourself no more than two weeks. By then if you don't understand what is going on, and if most of the other students seem to be engaged in the material, you are in trouble. It's time to drop this course.

Take action quickly, before it is too late. Some students go through most of a semester, realizing that their work is not going well but not doing anything about it. They stay in all their courses past the last date when they can drop a class, and do miserably in all of them. Other students will drop one or two courses at the last possible minute, but by then they have lost all the time and effort that they spent on the uncompleted courses.

Don't wait until the last date to drop a class. Make the decision to switch courses early in the semester. You not only want to handle the work you take on, but to do it well.

NOT ENOUGH MONEY?

Almost all graduate students have money problems, but if yours become so severe that you are not sure you can continue, talk to your department's Graduate Adviser. Tell him or her honestly what the situation is and see if you can get any help. Ask about fellowships or assistantships. If you already have an assistantship, ask if you can work more hours. Departments have a lot of flexibility in the way that they assign teaching. For the next term, you might be able to teach more hours and get more money.

He or she may have additional suggestions. Perhaps there are jobs around your department. Ask in your department's office if there is seasonal office work you can do. You might be able to tutor students or help a faculty member's research.

Then try the university's office of financial aid. See what you are offered. There may be some assistantships for graduate students that are not tied to any academic department, perhaps in an administrative office. Maybe you are eligible for a work-study job.

Next, investigate loans, but if you do take out a student loan or increase the amount you are borrowing, check out the terms and see if the interest you will have to pay starts piling up from the day you get your loan, or if it is a subsidized loan for which you won't be charged interest while you are in school. Student loans are covered in Chapter 4.

Last, if really necessary, look at outside jobs. But if you do take another job, be sure to give your academic work top priority. It's bad economics to spend too much time on a low-paying job and stretch out the years you have to be in school; it's better to scrimp.

BEWARE OF CREDIT CARDS

You will get offers while you are in school. Some of them sound too good to turn down, particularly when you are strapped for cash and can hardly buy anything once you pay for food and shelter. But resist them; you don't want to end up thousands of dollars in debt to a credit card company and spend your time dodging bill collectors. The money you borrow for your academic program is paying for your education, something that will last your life. What you buy on credit usually does not.

Educational loans are worthwhile; credit card debt is not. The credit card companies want their interest right away, and the interest charges are very steep. Remember, missing even a few credit card payments can ruin your credit rating for years to come.

George and his wife Emmy learned that lesson too late. After months of threatening letters and telephone calls and many sleepless nights, they had to ask his parents for help in paying off some of their credit card debts. It was embarrassing, and also meant that they didn't feel they could ask his family for help in paying back their student loans.

HEALTH INSURANCE

You should check out your health insurance. Many universities require all students to use (and pay for) a student health insurance plan. Sometimes these plans are very good, and will cover such services as stress reduction programs and physical therapy. You are paying for this coverage; take advantage of it. At universities that don't have universal student coverage, if you are a teaching or research assistant, or a fellow, you may have health insurance through your job or fellowship. And if you don't have a job you can probably take out insurance through the university. It's a good idea to do so.

However, if you only have student insurance, it may lapse in the summer if you are not taking any courses. The university may have a plan that allows you to extend your student insurance over the summer. If not, think about getting some auxiliary insurance, particularly if you have children; the trouble is, it is often so expensive that students take their chances without it.

This is not a good idea because you can't predict when an accident will occur, with a physical and financial aftermath that may continue for years.

Because Nan was healthy, she thought health insurance was not important. She loved sports and the outdoors until the day she was skiing on the intermediate slope. A five-year-old boy in front of her stopped suddenly; to avoid him, she swerved and fell. Her minimal health insurance only paid partly for the orthopedic surgery, and she needed almost a year of physical therapy before she could walk again without a cane and get back to full-time graduate work. It was a serious financial blow.

CHOOSING A THESIS DIRECTOR

For many students, next to the choice of program, the most important decision is choosing a thesis director or adviser. It's really crucial for doctoral students. When you start school, you are usually assigned to a professor who will give you advice about courses and requirements, but choosing a thesis director is different; this is a close, long-term relationship.

For each student who is writing a thesis, an individual committee of faculty members is formed to guide that student and eventually to approve the thesis. The thesis director is usually the chair of this committee. For a master's thesis the committee can be appointed by the department head, but a doctoral committee may have to be approved by the Graduate College of the university. Almost all of the student's contact is with the thesis director, but other members of the committee may occasionally be asked for help on some aspect of the research. The committee is usually appointed after you have started work with your thesis director.

In some areas, such as engineering or chemistry, your adviser and thesis-director-to-be may have selected you as one of his or her students at the time you were admitted. Your offer may include a research assistantship with this professor, and in accepting the offer you have accepted that professor as your adviser.

Or, in other programs, you have to choose your adviser and probable thesis director within the first few weeks. If, for example, you are a chemistry doctoral student who accepts a research assistantship in your professor's lab, it will be difficult to make a change. This can put you under a lot of pressure.

In the liberal arts or social sciences, you probably will not know the specific area you will work on until you are well into your program. This gives you time to look around and see which faculty member is responsible for certain fields, for instance, in history, early Victorian England or colonial Spain. Find out about the professor in the area you are interested in and his or her treatment of students before you decide.

It's not so vital if you are working on a master's thesis, but still you will have to work closely with your adviser for months, and you will want good advice, guidance, and, when you complete the degree, recommendations.

As a doctoral student, your adviser is of major importance, since the joint work may go on for years, and after graduation you will initially be known as a student of Professor Jones.

A GOOD ADVISER

You want someone you can see who:

- will keep appointments;
- is interested in you and your progress;

- will help you;
- will suggest what you can do when you get stuck and not let you flounder around for years;
- is glad that you are moving ahead;
- doesn't make one unreasonable demand after another, thus delaying you;
- will try to get funds for you;
- will help you get a job; and
- has a reputation good enough so that a recommendation from that person will help to start you in the field.

This information about faculty members is difficult to find out. You probably know who are the big names in the department, but not every student is going to have a big-name adviser. Talk to fellow students who are working on their dissertations; see what they have to say about their advisers. A faculty member may not have a big reputation, but still might be someone who is very effective, who helps students write a good thesis and get good jobs. It is not easy to predict if someone will encourage and support you, but you should definitely try to do so. Observe the faculty. See how they deal with students and with each other. Find out what their former students are doing now.

A real problem occurs if you have gotten to the stage of writing a thesis, and you can't work with your chosen thesis director. The best defense against this is to be careful in your choice of a director, but sometimes a student, through faults on one or both sides, can't continue with the adviser he or she chose. If this happens, try to cut your losses as soon as possible. When you see trouble looming on the horizon, begin to look for another adviser. Try to find a sympathetic faculty member in a closely related area. This professor might agree to take you as a student, or at least advise you on what to do.

When it came time for John to choose an adviser, he was thinking about the different possibilities, Professor A or Professor B, both of whom were well known and recognized by their peers for their outstanding mathematical research. One day he was in Professor B's office when the telephone rang and the professor was asked about a former student of his. Professor B exclaimed in such glowing detail and spoke so enthusiastically of his former student that on the spot John decided to ask him to become his adviser. Several years later, when he got his first job, he knew he had made the right decision.

HOW YOU CAN FIND OUT THE TRUTH

Your program will undoubtedly have a list of all past graduates together with their thesis titles and the names of their advisers. You can ask at the office of the Graduate Adviser to see such a list. You will have to be tactful because faculty members don't really like the idea of graduate students comparing them. Say that you want to see from the thesis titles what past students worked on, so if you have similar interests you can talk to that professor. You will find that some faculty members have a steady stream of students; others have very few.

Johanna advises getting to know the people in the Graduate Adviser's office. She says, "They know a great deal about faculty/student relations, as well as everything else you might need help with." She goes on, "While they probably won't answer a question like 'Is Professor Jones awful to his students?', discreet questioning can get you far."

There is probably a professional association for your field with a directory that gives names, addresses, and professional affiliations. You can look up former students to see where they are now and how they have progressed in the real world. One professor's students might be doing well; another's might not even be in the directory.

Talk to students who are studying with a faculty member you might want for your adviser. Are the students making progress, finishing up their degrees? Some faculty members have a reputation for rarely letting their students actually finish a dissertation. There is always new information to put in, or revisions to be made. No student should have to undergo years of work on a dissertation and end up not getting the degree.

Strange as it seems, some of these impossible advisers continue to get new students.

Whatever you do, don't choose a thesis director without talking to everyone you can, and doing a little research.

HOW LUCY COPED WITH A BAD ADVISER

While Lucy was in graduate school working for her Ph.D., her first adviser was hired away by another university; so was her second. She had several advisers. One was a famous person whom many students wanted to work with. But as she says, "What matters is not whether the person is famous or not. What you want is an adviser who is willing to work for you, one who will do what is required."

When the adviser she ended up with turned out to be only interested in furthering his own career and getting an offer from a more prestigious university, Lucy found a professor from another department, a woman whose interests matched hers. With permission from her own department, Lucy asked her to be co-chair of her doctoral committee, and in effect, be her thesis adviser. "I would advise any student stuck with an adviser who is not so good to see if the department will let you get a co-chair from another unit and then find someone who will help you," she says.

Lucy managed to do an end run around the non-performing adviser from her own department, who became a co-chair instead of the chair of her thesis committee. The real advising was done by the co-chair from the other department. Most students do not have to go to such Byzantine lengths to get good advice.

As she sees it, "The end result of graduate school is to get a job. Persevere," she says, "and learn how to market yourself so you look like someone who will be able to make an impact in the field." Lucy was in comparative literature, so she was able to find an adviser in a different department. If you are in geology, it won't be that easy. You may be able to change advisers inside the department, but you will have to be careful to avoid having an influential professor angry with you.

A university, like any human institution, is a political place, and if you think that you are not very good at playing politics, this is a good opportunity to refine your skills. It may take nothing more than sitting down, thinking about who has the potential to help you along, and then making sure that in all your interactions with those people you pay careful attention to the cues that they give you. For example, the Graduate Adviser may not tell you directly that you are taking too much of her time, but you will be able to sense her annoyance if that is the case.

TEST ANXIETY

One thing is certain about graduate school: You will have to take lots of tests. If examinations make you anxious, you are not unusual. In a challenging situation, being keyed up is good; it will get more adrenaline flowing and will probably help you to do better.

But some people get so panicky when they have to take an examination that the tension causes them to freeze, and their minds stop functioning so that they cannot answer even the questions they know. In acute cases, you stare at the exam, unable to focus, and realize that your mind has become a blank.

If you suffer from test anxiety, you know it is a real condition. You get into a state where your heart beats faster, your pulse speeds up, and hormones are secreted that trigger other reactions. You may sweat more, or suffer from headaches or stomachaches. Your field of vision narrows and becomes tunnellike, leaving you with little peripheral sight.

If this has happened to you, you are not alone; many others suffer from test anxiety, and there are things you can do to ease it.

The first step is to learn to relax. Try your student health center first. There you will probably find books or tapes that tell you how to relax. See about counseling. All universities have counselors who will work with students, either individually or in a workshop about common problems. And test anxiety is one. Some workshops will cover several potential problem areas such as stress reduction, career and study counseling, physical therapy and diet counseling. Others will focus on test anxiety.

Learn and practice relaxation methods before your next exam. If before or during the examination you start to panic, stretch as hard as you can, tensing the muscles in your arms and legs; then suddenly relax all of them. This will help relieve tension. Take deep, slow breaths.

One way to avoid panic in the exam is to keep your class work up to date and not leave too much studying to the last minute.

It helps to study with others. In one plant identification class, before the exams a group of horticulture students would all get together and make up silly mnemonics in order to remember the Latin names. When the exam started, they found this tactic had been very helpful.

Also, think to yourself and ask each other, What questions are likely to be asked? What was emphasized in class? Every course has a basic structure, and if you understand the fundamental ideas it will be easier to guess what will be on the exam. Go over the textbook, making notations. Also review your class notes and any papers you have written for the course as well as any earlier exams, paying attention to the professor's remarks.

Other suggestions on coping with test anxiety were given in Chapter 8.

PEOPLE PROBLEMS

Nobody is perfect, and sometimes you will have contact with other students who cause problems. Sometimes you are thrown in contact with an irritating person. You don't have to be in graduate school for this to happen, but in that situation it may take on more serious overtones.

Joni had arrived with a fellowship, and was irritated when her fellow student David implied that women were given preference over men in fellowship awards. David finally stated as a fact that the department favored women over men both in admissions and awards. She went to the Graduate Adviser and asked if this was true. After he denied it, she told him what David had been saying. He called in David, explained how the process of admissions and awards worked, and asked him how he could say that there was favoritism. David mumbled something vague, and then, referring to himself in the third person, said, "David could never be sexist." Whatever was going on inside his head, he did stop making such remarks.

This was a minor problem, but Joni was right to make a complaint. This kind of rumor can damage a department.

Graduate school can put people under a lot of pressure, and people sometimes develop serious problems as a result.

William, who was a graduate student in chemistry, realized that a fellow student, Ben, was becoming increasingly depressed and was drinking laboratory alcohol in the lab they shared. It made him uneasy, but he kept telling himself, "It's not my business."

One day when William was working on his experiment he heard the pop of a gun. He turned and saw Ben waving a pistol. "I hope those are blanks," William said. Instead of answering, Ben aimed the gun at him and shot William twice in the chest. William was taken to the hospital, where fortunately he recovered, although he still has a bullet lodged inside him.

William realized that he should have told his adviser that Ben's behavior was becoming strange. He had seen Ben sitting for hours, not speaking, moving, or working, then a few minutes later flying into a rage, swearing and muttering and banging around the laboratory equipment.

William hadn't wanted to interfere or say something bad about a fellow student. He knew too late that he should have. He was a sensible person and would have been taken seriously.

After a hearing, Ben was sent to a mental institution in another state. This was a little late for William's well-being.

MINOR TROUBLES

Few students become so unbalanced that they shoot others, but you may experience minor annoyances. If you are having trouble with an office mate, find out who controls the office assignments and ask that your office be changed. If you are asked why, simply say that you are worried about possible conflict with an office mate and want to avoid any difficulty. You may have to wait for the end of the school year, but you will feel a lot better if relief is in sight.

Do your best to avoid disputes with other members of your department. If you get into an argument with a faculty member, some of the faculty will automatically take their colleague's side. If your disagreement is with a student, faculty members will not want to be drawn into it.

HELP NEEDED

When a difficult situation arises, anyone intelligent enough to be in graduate school can stop and try to decide on the best course of action. You can also ask experienced graduate students what they do when they have difficulty and decide whether what they say is right for you in the circumstances. A sympathetic faculty member may give you good advice, but some faculty members are quite ignorant about administrative procedures, don't know what to do, and don't want to be involved.

Many departments have an administrative secretary who knows everything that is going on. Lucy, who got her Ph.D. in comparative literature, says that all graduate students should make friends with the department secretary and other nonfaculty staff. They can be very helpful, often will tell you something you need to know, and may even turn out to be valuable allies.

Marie, an older student who planned to go back to work on a master's in sociology, read the requirements for a graduate degree and thought that she would be required to take the GRE Subject Examination in sociology in addition to the general exam. One day she dropped into the department office and was talking to the secretary about the GRE. She found out that no recent applicants had taken the GRE Subject Exam and that they had been admitted without it. The department brochure was out of date, and she learned to her great relief, even though no one had bothered to tell all the new applicants, that now the subject exam was not required. This saved her not only money and time, but the additional stress.

*   *   *

In all your dealings with faculty or administrators in your department, it is important to be as reasonable as you can and not to make frivolous requests. People will then usually be glad to help you.

For example, there is usually a reason for something that happens in your department. You may not think it is a good reason, but others may disagree.

Edward was a graduate student with fairly rigid ideas about how things should be done. His job as a TA was to grade papers in Professor Watson's class. One Thursday, Watson gave Edward a sheaf of student papers and told Edward that Friday's class was canceled, since he would be out of town, and the papers were to be graded by Monday morning. Edward threw the papers down on Watson's desk and refused to grade them. This led to an interview with the Associate Head. Edward told him that it was immoral for a professor to skip a class and that he wanted nothing to do with it. The Associate Head told Edward that it was not his job to set moral standards for the profession; his job was to grade papers, and if he refused, another student could be found to do the job. Edward graded the papers. The only thing he accomplished was to get himself known as something of a crackpot.

TROUBLED STUDENTS

Very few students crack up to the extent that Ben did, talking audibly to himself as he walked through the halls, often in a state of rage. Long before people reach the point where they start complaining that other graduate students and faculty are conspiring to prevent them from finishing their work, they should get help or have it thrust upon them.

Another troubled graduate student was Stanley, who shared an office with Timmy. Stanley was 6 foot 4, a weight lifter, a foot taller than Timmy, and about 50 pounds heavier. One day Stanley exploded, accused Timmy of using up his coffee, and grabbed him around the neck.

"I'll kill you," he said, "if you do that again."

Timmy panicked and ran out of the office. The police were called, but no charges were pressed. Stanley, who had not been taking his medication, resumed taking it and became a rational person again. Before he left at the end of the semester to continue his studies elsewhere, Stanley said to his adviser, "Tim shouldn't have called the police. When I grabbed him, he should have decked me."

"But," the adviser said, "you are much stronger. Suppose he had tried and failed." Stanley thought a minute and replied, "Then there might have been some trouble."

There had already been enough trouble for Timmy, who departed and spent a term at another school 200 miles away. He returned only after Stanley had left.

Timmy's reaction may seem a little excessive and may have cost him some time, but he is still with us. Certainly he could have gotten support from the department, but this may have seemed inadequate when he was being throttled by a 200-pound maniac.

OTHER PROBLEMS

There are some problems you don't need, such as being caught cheating. To avoid that, don't cheat.

Undergraduates sometimes think that cheating is no big deal. Many of them cheat when they have the opportunity, and most are not caught. But cheating in graduate school is a different matter. If you are caught copying an exam or turning in someone else's work as your own, you can wreck your academic career before it starts.

Another problem area is dating. If you are a teaching assistant, you should never date a current student of yours. If you can't put that person out of mind, wait until the term is over and the grades have been assigned, so there is no hint of irregularity. And the same thing applies, in reverse, to dating a professor. It's better not to date the faculty, but if you do, it should be a person who has no connection whatever with your work. In your own department, stay away socially from faculty members anywhere near your area. You might want to take their classes, or you could find them on a committee that is important to you. Social relations that have gone sour can present a massive problem.

Sometimes a student will look on the department secretaries as servants. It is a bad idea to treat the clerical help as if they are inferiors. They think they are just as good as you are. They are, and if they complain about your behavior, it will be taken seriously. If you can't make friends with them, don't make enemies.

A DIFFICULT PROFESSOR

Sometimes a student gets into an impossible situation.

Julie finished her course work and was working on her dissertation in American literature with a charismatic professor who, she knew, liked her. He was a leader in the field, he had many publications and professional honors, and she respected his work. During the winter of her third year, he invited her to have dinner with him and his wife as he had occasionally done before. When she arrived at his house, he said that his wife had been called out of town. Previously other students had also been invited to dinner, but that night no one else arrived. She was uneasy. "But, after all," she told herself, "he is an old man, at least 60."

She didn't want to hurt his feelings, but she did not like it when he stroked her hand and wanted to put his arm around her. She left early, glad that she had escaped before anything else happened. It was all very upsetting. She wondered if somehow she had done something wrong and given him the impression that she was a woman who welcomed his attention. She definitely was not.

From then on he found more occasions for her to come to his office and to touch her and to talk to her, about subjects other than the dissertation. He was becoming very unprofessional.

She didn't know what to do. He found more opportunities to be with her. She went to a counselor who told her to write down what happened and on what day. She began to keep a record in a little notebook. No matter what she said, he didn't stop. Again she went to the counselor, who advised her to write him a letter telling him she did not like his attentions and to please stop.

He answered her letter with one of his own, telling her that he could help her professionally, but that if she didn't continue working with him it would be difficult for her to get an academic position.

She felt trapped in this situation, but she knew she couldn't stay as his student.

She left to go to another adviser, a woman faculty member interested in women's literature, who told her she must file an official complaint.

Reluctantly, Julie did. The professor was reprimanded, was told not to have any more female graduate students, and suffered a tremendous loss of prestige in his department. Julie lost time, made an enemy, and had to change her research area.

Sexual harassment is less common now than it was since professors have become more sensitive and realize that it is taken very seriously by the universities. But it does happen. If you feel you are becoming a victim, immediately talk to a counselor to find out what you should do.

POOR TEACHING

Some professors are boring. While universities are paying more attention now to whether or not their professors are good at teaching, professors are hired primarily for their research and their contributions to their field, not for their teaching ability.

Most faculty members are excited about their subject, but not all are excited about students. It's difficult for even the best students to catch the excitement if the professor has no interest in them. A good student needs a good faculty member. Your fellow students can help you find professors who are good teachers and are willing to talk to students.

Just because someone is a famous historian or a computer science whiz does not mean he or she will be a good teacher. A well-known mathematician couldn't even keep himself awake while he was teaching. One day in class when he was writing equations on the blackboard, he leaned against the board in the corner of the room to rest. A few moments later he suddenly started, realizing that he had fallen asleep and was sliding down the wall. For once his students were wide awake; they were watching with interest to see if he would actually fall to the floor.

Boring people are a fact of life. If a faculty member is known for tedious classes, you can try to take the same course with someone else, but if you need that class and there is no other way to get it, and it is only taught by someone who is a total bore, just remember it is not the end of the world. It will be over in a few months. And resolve now that you will never, ever be that kind of a teacher.

THINKING ABOUT DROPPING OUT?

Often, after the challenge of starting this new life, people find that being a graduate student involves a lot of hard work and their excitement ebbs away. This is particularly true of some doctoral students whose goal begins to seem impossibly far off. They begin to have doubts. They wonder if they can do it, if it is worth it. It is.

Keep on, and usually any temporary depression you feel will lift. If it doesn't, talk to a counselor at the student clinic. Counselors have dealt with this problem many times. As you get accustomed to being a graduate student and learn how things are done in your department, you will learn how to manage your time. Graduate school will get easier.

Occasionally, after they are in the program, people find out that their interests really have changed. The classes are not what they thought they would be. The work is not interesting or stimulating.

Almost all students who drop out before finishing are intelligent enough to do the work. The trouble is that they have lost interest.

When Nat was a senior at Columbia University, his professor, who was delighted with his work in French, told him there was a fellowship at Yale in French literature. Because he liked the books he was reading in French and because he did not have anything else in mind, Nat applied, and with the recommendation of his professor received the fellowship. Soon after he started at Yale, he learned he would have to take Latin and German and also learn medieval French. He attended the classes, hoping he would get more interested. He did not.

As the months passed and he plodded to class he realized that he did not care about any of these arcane subjects, and his conviction grew that this was not what he wanted to do. He stayed until the end of the academic year, then resigned his fellowship and went to Paris to study film making.

Some students lose interest but stay in school for several years more, and then drop out. This is not a good idea. If you have given it a good try and are convinced that you don't like being there, be prepared to change your goals and leave school. It is not sensible to continue, year after year, working on a degree because you are too stubborn to stop. Perhaps after some time away you will come back and restart. Or perhaps you will be happy doing something completely different.

Graduate school may not be what you expected. If you have tried to make a go of it and are sure that your interests have changed, it's foolish to march doggedly on toward a goal that no longer appeals to you. It's no disgrace not to have an M.S. in geology or a Ph.D. in psychology. Most people in the world live happy lives without one.

HELP AVAILABLE

Other problems involve family. Sometimes even after you make good arrangements and everything seems okay, something blows up in your face. While you plan as carefully as you can, it is not possible to predict every eventuality. Miserable spouses, children whose care has to be arranged, or parents who need help can derail your work. These are serious problems and can't be ignored. Sometimes you have to put your academic work on hold for a short time and devote yourself to working through these unhappy situations. But you can come back to it.

Before your life gets too messed up, see if there is something you can do about it. Talk to your adviser. Be quite honest about whatever is troubling you. Or, if you prefer, find a counselor to talk to. A good counselor has probably seen many situations such as yours and should have some insights. At the least, a counselor can tell you where to go for help.

You have already passed the first test. You were selected by the admissions committee as a person with talent and intelligence who can do the work and get a good degree. You have started graduate school and survived the difficult first weeks of being in a new and demanding environment, unlike any you have been in before. You can do it. If problems arise, you can solve them. You are on your way, and you are going to do well.

CHAPTER 13

FOR THE **RETURNING STUDENT**

> **W**hen my husband was in graduate school, we needed my salary. Then I raised my family and worked in another office. Finally I decided to reward myself and get a master's degree in history, a subject I loved and never had time to pursue. It was the smartest thing I ever did. At first I wondered what it would be like being in class with all those people younger than my children. It was great.
>
> *—URSULA*

AN **INCREASING NUMBER** of people who go to graduate school have been out of college for several years or even longer. They want to change their lives around, to take up something completely different, or to advance in their present careers. If you have been away from school for quite a while, you have a life. You have a circle of friends, work of some kind, perhaps a family. It may be difficult to make the break and take on something so unlike what you have been doing. Even if you don't care for your work, you have a routine you are used to, people you work with. You may be giving up your current career and an income, or possibly you plan to keep your job and go to school part time, taking on the tasks of being in school in addition to your work.

Of course, those circumstances will not apply to everyone. Perhaps you have been staying home with children for several years, and they are now in school so you have time to think about your own education. Perhaps you were "downsized" from your job and have some severance pay. In any case, you would not even think of graduate school if you were satisfied with your situation. Still, the decision is going to involve more life changes for you than for the recent graduate.

First, you will have to go through the admission procedures, the application form, the recommendations and transcripts, the GRE or other tests and—what frightens many people—you will have to write the essay. See the earlier chapters that deal with all of these tasks.

Then, when you are accepted and in school, you will be attending classes and taking notes while the professors lecture, reading required textbooks, studying for and sitting for examinations and writing term papers, all tasks you probably have not done for years. Just keep in mind that you can do it, although it may take a little time to get accustomed to the new routine.

BACK TO SCHOOL

A returning student has some natural advantages. If you are older than other students, you have had longer to become acquainted with yourself and know your own strengths and weaknesses. What you can do is build on your strengths.

In graduate and professional programs, older, nontraditional students usually do very well because they:

- are responsible;
- are serious about their studies;
- are accustomed to working and accomplishing what has to be done;
- know how to budget their time and not to waste it;
- have been out in the world and have varied life experiences;
- have dealt with different people and can see others' points of view; and
- are patient.

Woody Allen said that 90 percent of life is showing up. A large part of success in graduate school, though maybe not 90 percent, consists in doing your work thoroughly and on time. If you have had a position with any responsibility, you will be used to this rule of life. An amazing number of undergraduate students put things off, turn in incomplete or incorrect work late, and often do not "show up." Most of these people do not go on to graduate school, but those who do don't magically change their spots during the summer after receiving their bachelor's degrees.

IN SOME FIELDS, OLDER STUDENTS ARE PREFERRED

Linda was older and had worked and raised a family when she decided to return to school for a master's in social work. When she went to visit the university, she found out that the dean preferred older students, people with work experience. The dean told her that mature students often did better in the program than the new graduates, who were too immature, too inexperienced.

Linda is a tall, handsome woman with a ready smile who looks more competent than she feels. She is reliable and knows how to work with people, but after years during which her reading consisted of mystery stories, and the only writing she had done was an occasional letter, she wasn't sure she'd be able to study and write examinations. Her nine-year-old son was not happy at being uprooted and moved from Massachusetts to the university town in Indiana. It took months before he made friends and stopped complaining.

The first year was not easy. After many years away from the academic life, reading textbooks, taking notes on what she read so that she could remember it and writing term papers were skills she had to relearn. But she wanted that degree, and she did not give up.

One thing that didn't faze her the way it did the younger students was speaking out in class. She had talked to so many people in her career that she wasn't afraid. In fact, she enjoyed talking. Linda, like many experienced social workers, wanted to share what she had learned on the job, and spoke out in class many times about her own experiences, not aware that sometimes older students monopolize class discussions.

After the professor cautioned her against talking too much, Linda learned to watch herself and hold back so that the others could have their turns to speak.

As she got accustomed to it, the academic program became easier. Linda received her M.S.W., which gave her an edge over others working in her field. Now she teaches potential social workers at a local community college.

BEING OLDER

Having experience gives you an advantage in other programs besides social work, such as law, or the master's degree in psychiatric nursing. Many M.B.A. programs will not consider admitting you until you have had work experience.

Some programs don't accept students older than a certain age. Most medical schools prefer younger students, reasoning that so many years have to be spent before a doctor becomes qualified that, after finishing, only a younger person would have the necessary years left to practice. If you want a medical career but are older, see if there is an allied field that you would be interested in, such as working for a Ph.D. in anatomy or physiology.

But while most academic programs may not look for mature students, neither do they discriminate against people who are older. Some departments may welcome younger students more enthusiastically because they think those students have more years ahead of them to contribute to the field. But if potential students have the qualifications, the grades, good test scores and recommendations, then they have a chance of being admitted, no matter how old they are. It is up to them to show they can do it.

When she was thirty, Erica started to think it was time to finish her education and get her graduate degree in psychology. But at first the thought frightened her. Even if she could arrange good child care for her two small children and get time to go to class and to study, she was terrified that she wouldn't be able to do the work. She didn't think she could face failure.

Afraid that she couldn't succeed, she resisted the idea, but finally she applied and was accepted.

Erica is tiny and was very shy. At first she never dared to take part in class discussions or go to the office and ask a professor for help. Studying for exams was as difficult as she had feared it would be.

When she was required to do a term paper, she couldn't even decide what topic to write on. Days would pass while the deadline got nearer and nearer. Instead of working she sat frozen in indecision, fretting and staring at the blank white paper. Suddenly, the night before the paper was due, she would snatch some topic, any topic, out of the air and write feverishly all night, then turn in the paper and get a much worse grade than she was capable of earning if she had started earlier. Gradually, she found that she could do the work. When she heard what the other students said in class discussions and began to get A's on her exams and term papers, she realized that the others were not any more intelligent than she was.

IF SHE HAD KNOWN THEN

Erica says that if she had known then what she learned later, her graduate school experience could have been much easier. If she were starting now, she says, she would enroll in a noncredit course in how to study and how to use her time effectively. She would become familiar with the computer and learn how to use the library on campus, and when the situation at home was troubling, she would go to a counselor for emotional support.

In two ways Erica was lucky. She could afford the tuition, and she lived in a town where she could attend the university and so did not have to uproot herself. Family relationships and finances are two of the biggest worries of many graduate students, particularly older ones. But Erica still had to rearrange her time and reschedule her life so that she could be a full-time student. She made it. Now she is one of the partners in a psychological counseling clinic.

Sometimes you find the program you have started is not for you. And then, knowing yourself can help so that you don't waste years.

Meredith began as a graduate student in sociology, but at the beginning of her second term realized that much of the sociology department's emphasis at that university was on statistics and numerical factors. Being aware of her own interests and her strong points, she realized that the quantitative emphasis in that department was not for her. Even though it meant she would have to spend more time in graduate school, she applied to transfer and was admitted as a candidate for a master's in the history department. There she was much happier.

She enjoyed going to class and reading the textbooks and even liked writing term papers. Before she knew it, she had earned her master's, had a new job, and was almost sorry that she would not be going to those interesting classes any longer.

SPECIAL PROBLEMS

There are some points to consider and a few special problems for returning students. Make your academic work your top priority. After being away from school for many years, it is extremely important to relearn good study habits. Primarily this means doing the work as it is assigned, not letting it pile up undone. Also, it means reading assignments *before* class so you have a clear idea of the day's topic and can take part in any classroom discussion, and doing a thorough job on any papers assigned. If optional reading or optional problems to solve are offered, it is a good idea to do them, to establish yourself as one of the better students.

Sometimes there will be more work than you can do at your best level. In that case, choose one or two courses for your maximum effort. These should be courses in which you are particularly interested, and want the instructor to know you and appreciate your work. Keep in mind that you will be relying on your professors for recommendations. A recommendation from an influential professor is much better than one from a routine teacher of required courses.

Some requirements may seem pointless, such as passing a test in reading a foreign language when you are pretty sure you will never use the language afterward, but if it is a requirement, unless you can get an official excuse in writing, you had better do it.

Also, take part in departmental activities. Attend coffee hours and department colloquia, serve on graduate or department committees. You may hesitate because you think that you are different from other students. The more you are active in the department, the more you will be accepted. If you just go to class and don't take part in other ways, you will become more isolated.

Some older students have not used computers and are uneasy about them, particularly when they have to take an important test such as the GRE on them. If you are not familiar with computers, learn as much as you can about them. Take a short course or ask a knowledgeable friend to show you how to use one. If you are not already familiar with one, learn how to use a word processor, a great time saver and almost essential for writing and printing out papers.

There are a few faculty members who want to be so identified with the undergraduates that they do not welcome older students. Meredith found this out when she went to back to school. Each term before she enrolled in a class, she would go to the faculty member's office and ask questions about the course contents. She thought she could tell right away if that person did not want an older student in the class. One term she went to speak to a young woman, who was becoming known for her books on the economic history of women, about taking her course, which was open to both graduate students and undergraduates. The young professor said that she felt it was her job primarily to work with younger people. Meredith could tell that she was not welcome in that class and wisely did not enroll in it.

There are some ways to make the transition to being a student easier on yourself. Take noncredit courses in study skills and time management. Almost all universities offer such courses, either free or for a reasonable fee. Try to arrange your courses according to your biological clock. If you are a morning person and open your eyes eager to go, but wilt later on, take your most demanding courses early in the day.

Other people find that they are more alert in certain seasons than in others and learn better at those times. Katie hated courses in the spring. She tried to do a lot of her teaching, and took her own most difficult courses, in the winter when the weather was bad anyway, so in spring she didn't have to work so hard. Fortunately for her, Minnesota was on the quarter system, so she could do this.

WHAT KATIE DID

If you have been accustomed to creature comforts and have some possessions that you really like, bring them along, even if it costs extra to move them. It's surprising how much a familiar chair or pictures can make a person feel less stressed.

When she left California, even though the moving costs were high, Katie brought not only her books and her computer but also pictures, rugs, chairs and small furniture, and linens. During the dark Minnesota winter when she grieved for the sun in her native California, her familiar belongings were a great comfort. She would come home from class, chilled right through her coat, her fingers in their gloves feeling like chunks of ice, her feet, despite her boots, hurting from the cold, and open her door. As she stepped inside, warmth surrounded her and she sank down on her own cushions, looking at her own pictures on the wall. "It really helped," she said. "It gave me a little feeling of coming home, and that made it possible to work instead of sitting around feeling bereft."

If you have worked and been treated like a responsible adult, you will find that as a graduate student at times you will not be. Unfortunately, students, even graduate students, are sometimes treated like a lower form of life by faculty and administrators. People in positions of authority may be brusque, or even downright rude. Some faculty members do not think your time is as valuable as theirs. They will schedule office hours and not show up. If you have worked in the adult world, you may have forgotten this attitude toward students that some people have. It will take some getting used to, and you will sometimes have to politely point out that you are not being treated well.

BEING RESPONSIBLE

If you are doing any kind of work for your department, your maturity will be an advantage for you. Whether you work as a TA, as a grader, in the library, or even in the mail room, a mature approach to work will help you. Departmental administrators are all too familiar with workers who don't show up or who don't take their jobs seriously. It's a pleasure for an administrator to appoint a student to some position knowing that the job will be done thoroughly and well.

After serving in the Air Force and working four years as an engineer, Frank started work on his Ph.D. in mathematics. He felt that people did not treat him as a full adult, even though he was twenty-nine years old, but automatically classified him as "student," with its connotations of immaturity and impulsiveness. It takes time to show people, by your work and your behavior, that you are all grown up.

Frank was a good teacher rather than an inspiring one, but unlike some of the less mature teaching assistants, he prepared his classes thoroughly so he gave clear lectures on difficult areas of mathematics, and he graded homework and tests promptly so he could return students' papers and turn in the grades to the department on time. He also kept the office hours he had scheduled and met his students. His department recognized he was dependable and responsible. By his third year he was appointed a predoctoral instructor, a cut above a TA. This position brought him more money and, when he earned his degree, that line on his resumé helped him get a job as an assistant professor.

A potential student once wrote to a newspaper columnist, "I'd like to go back to grad school but don't know if I should, because by the time I get my degree in four years I will be thirty-seven." The columnist wrote, "In four years you will be thirty-seven whether or not you get the degree."

If you are older, it may take longer to get accustomed to being back in school. But to Frank and to many other older students, graduate school was liberating. To have as his major task learning more in a field he found infinitely fascinating was great. He felt as if he was growing and understanding his area as a whole.

He went through difficult times, many days of stress and tension, before the all-important examinations, but graduate school was essential preparation for what he became—a professor at a major research university.

CHAPTER 14

CONCLUSION

A NEW LIFE

GRADUATE SCHOOL SHOULD be challenging; it can be difficult. Sometimes you may wonder why you are doing this and begin to doubt the whole business. Working toward a graduate degree is not always easy, but as you will learn, it is one of the most rewarding things you can do for yourself. Even though it may not be simple to make the transition to being a graduate student, the rewards are great.

WHAT PEOPLE SAY

When you talk to people who have completed a graduate program, almost always they say how glad they are that they did.

Pam had a bachelor's degree in English and was working as a secretary when she decided to go back to get a master's in education and a teaching certificate. She says, "It changed my life. I love it. Now I'm a teacher."

Others describe graduate school as stimulating, challenging, even exhilarating.

Jenny decided that she needed more medical knowledge after 20 years in massage therapy. She says one unexpected benefit she received along with her degree in physical therapy was the psychological boost. "My husband says I'm a different person now, more confident and interesting to be with."

Edgar, a 39-year-old accounts manager with AT&T who wanted to look beyond what he was doing and to learn more about technology, wasn't sure he could compete with younger students. Full of trepidation, he enrolled at the University of Rochester. He earned an A in calculus and B's in microeconomics and marketing. "I learned I could do it," he says triumphantly. "My horizons expanded."

If they can do it, you can.

Start in and go for it. You will be glad that you did. Charles, who went back to school after ten years out in the world, agrees. He says, "Keep on. You may get discouraged at times, but it is worth it. You will see."

REFERENCES

The addresses of many of these publishers and organizations are given below in the section on Reference Addresses.

GENERAL GUIDES

America's Best Graduate Schools, published annually by *U.S. News*, Washington, DC, $5.95. The current edition covers Business, Education, Engineering, Health, Law, and Medicine.

GRE/CGS Directory of Graduate and Professional Programs, 15th edition, Educational Testing Service, Princeton, NJ, 1995, $20.00 per volume. This directory is published in four volumes which cover different subject areas.

Guide to American Graduate Schools, 7th edition, by Harold R. Doughty, Penguin Books, New York, 1994, $23.95.

Peterson's Guide to Graduate and Professional Programs, Vols. 1–6, published annually by Peterson's, Princeton, NJ, prices from $27.95 to $44.95. This is an enormous set of volumes, giving information on virtually every graduate program.

Pursuit of the Ph.D., by William Bowen and Neil Rudenstine, Princeton University Press, NJ, 1992. A useful book, now out of print but available in libraries.

Student Guide to Research-Doctorate Programs, National Research Council, Washington, DC, 1996, $19.95. This is a condensed version of *Research-Doctorate Programs in the United States: Continuity and Change,* listed below in the section on rankings of programs.

GUIDES IN SPECIFIC DISCIPLINES

ABA Approved Law Schools, ed. Rick L. Morgan and Kurt Schneider, first edition, MacMillan, New York, 1998, $19.95. This is a complete list with information on all ABA-approved schools, prepared by the Section of Legal Education and Admissions to the Bar of the American Bar Association.

Barron's Guide to Graduate Business Schools, 9th edition, by Eugene Miller, Barron's Educational Services, Inc., Hauppage, NY, 1995, $14.95.

Barron's Guide to Law Schools, 12th edition, Barron's Educational Services, Inc., Hauppage, NY, 1996, $14.95. This guide includes schools that are not approved by the ABA, and discusses their disadvantages and advantages.

Barron's Guide to Medical and Dental Schools, 8th edition, by Saul Waschnitzer, Barron's Educational Services, Inc., Hauppage, NY, 1997, $16.95.

The Best___Schools, 1997, by Princeton Review, Random House, New York, 1998, $20.00. This series covers business, medical and law schools.

The Best Graduate Business Schools, 2nd edition, ed. Thomas Bachhuber, Macmillan, New York, 1996, $16.95.

Business Week Guide to the Best Business Schools, 5th edition, by John A. Byrne, McGraw-Hill, New York, 1997, $16.95.

Graduate Study in Psychology and Related Fields, American Psychological Association, Washington, DC 1996, $19.95.

Lovejoy's Guide to Graduate Programs in___, by Wintergreen, Macmillan General Ref., New York, 1997, $22.95. This series has books in Biological Sciences, Humanities and Social Sciences, and Engineering and Computer Science.

Medical School Admission Requirements, United States and Canada, 1999–2000, 49th edition, Association of American Medical Colleges, Washington, DC, 1998, $25.00.

The Official Guide to MBA Programs, Graduate Management Admissions Council, Princeton, NJ, 1994, $14.95.

The Official Guide to U.S. Law Schools, Law School Admission Council, Newtown, PA, 1998, $17.00.

Student Advantage Guide to the Best Graduate Programs in___, by Princeton Review, Random House, New York, 1997, $20.00 to $24.00. This series of books covers Engineering, Humanities and Social Sciences, and Physical and Biological Sciences.

Veterinary Medical Schools Admissions Requirements in the United States and Canada, Williams and Wilkins, Media, PA, 1996, $14.95. Sponsored by the Association of American Veterinary Medical Colleges and the Veterinary Medical Colleges Application Service. Over half of the colleges require applicants to use this service.

JOBS

Most big bookstores have a very large section of books on job hunting, opportunities, resumés, and all other aspects of the job search. We list only a few.

Career Choices for Students of___, revised editions, Walker and Company, New York, 1990, $8.95 to $9.95. There is a separate book for each of the fields: Art, Business, Communications and Journalism, Computer Science, Economics, English, History, Law, Mathematics, Political Science and Government, and Psychology.

Careers for Bookworms and other Literary Types, 2nd edition, by Marjorie Eberts and Margaret Gisler, NTC Contemp. Publishing Co., Lincolnwood, IL, 1995, $9.95.

Careers for Students of History, by Barbara J. Howe, American Historical Association, Washington, DC, 1989, $8.00.

Careers for Students of Science and Engineering: A Student Planning Guide to Graduate School and Beyond, National Research Council, Washington, DC, 1996, $11.95.

*Careers in*____. VGM Professional Careers Series, Lincolnwood, IL, 1994 to 1997, $13.95 to $17.95. There are separate books for Accounting, Advertising, Business, Child Care, Communications, Computers, Education, Engineering, Environment, Finance, Government, Health Care, High Tech, International Business, Journalism, Law, Marketing, Medicine, Science, and Social Science. This is a good series.

RANKINGS OF PROGRAMS (CHAPTER 3)

Some of these books are out of print, but since the relative quality of graduate programs changes so slowly, they are still interesting.

America's Best Graduate Schools. See entry under "General Guides."

An Assessment of Quality in Graduate Education, by A. M. Cartter, American Council on Education, Washington, DC, 1966. Out of print.

The Gourman Report: A Rating of Graduate and Professional Programs in American and International Universities, 7th edition revised, by Jack Gourman, National Educational Standards, Los Angeles, CA, 1996, $19.95.

A Rating of Graduate Programs, by K. Roose and C. Anderson, American Council on Higher Education, Washington, DC, 1970. Out of print.

Research-Doctorate Programs in the United States, Jones, Lindzey and Coggeshall, National Research Council Washington, DC, 1982 (the first NRC survey). Out of print.

Research-Doctorate Programs in the United States: Continuity and Change, ed. M. L. Goldberger, B. A. Maher, P. E. Flatteau, National Academy Press, Washington, DC, 1995, $59.95. This is an authoritative ranking of programs. It is a much enlarged update of the 1982 survey; it shows that the rankings of programs change surprisingly little.

Student Guide to Research-Doctorate Programs. See entry under "General Guides."

FINANCIAL AID (CHAPTER 4)

Annual Register of Grant Support 1998, edited by R. R. Bowker staff, Bowker, 1997, $199.95.

Financial Aid for Law School: A Preliminary Guide. Available free from the Law School Admission Council. For address see Reference Addresses.

Financing Graduate School, by P. McWade, Peterson's, Princeton, NJ, 1996, $16.95.

Financial Planning and Management Manual for U.S. Medical Students, Association of American Medical Colleges, Washington, DC, 1994, $7.50.

Free Money for Graduate School, 3rd edition, by Laurie Blum, Facts on File, Inc., New York, 1996, $15.95.

Grants Register, by Ruth Austin, St. Martin's Press, New York, 1997, $115.00.

Peterson's Grants for Graduate and Postdoctoral Study, 4th edition, Peterson, Princeton, NJ, 1994, $89.95.

The Prentice Hall Guide to Scholarships and Fellowships for Math and Science Students, by M. Kantrowitz and Joann P. DiGennaro, Prentice Hall, New York, 1993, $19.95.

The Student Guide: Financial Aid from the U.S. Department of Education, 1997–98. Available free from the Federal Student Aid Information Center, P.O. Box 84, Washington, DC 20044.

Worldwide Graduate Scholarship Directory, by Daniel J. Cassidy, Career Press, Franklin Lakes, NJ, 1995, $26.99.

TEST PREPARATION (CHAPTER 8)

Every big bookstore has a large number of test preparation books. Here are some that seem to be good.

GRE
The Best Test Preparation for the GRE General Test, Research and Education Association, Piscataway, NJ, 1990, $19.95.

The Best Test Preparation for the GRE in Subject____, Research and Education Association, Piscataway, NJ, 1995 to 1997, $22.95 to $27.95.

Available for many of the subject tests, these books are by a consortium of thirteen authors, and include real tests to practice on.

Cracking the GRE, by Adam Robinson, Random House, New York, 1997, $29.95. Sponsored by the Princeton Review.

Practicing to Take the GRE General Test—Big Book, by The Educational Testing Service, Warner Books, New York, 1996, $30.00.

Practicing to Take the GRE ____Test, by The Educational Testing Service, Warner Books, 1987 to 1997, $9.00 to $15.00. These books are available for many of the subject tests.

Princeton Review: Inside the GRE, by Princeton Review, Random House, New York, 1996, $36.95, (CD-ROM included).

OTHER TESTS

ARCO publishes a series of test preparation books for the GRE, GMAT, LSAT, MAT, and MCAT.

Barron's publishes a series of books giving preparation for every significant examination.

The Kaplan Organization, tel. 800 KAP-TEST, offers preparation courses for the GRE and almost all other tests.

The Princeton Review, tel. 800 2-REVIEW, offers preparation courses for GRE, GMAT, LSAT, MAT, and MCAT.

LSAT: The Official Triple Prep Plus with Explanations, Law School Admissions Council, Newtown, PA, $16.00. The LSAC publishes various LSAT preparation books, listed in the *LSAT & LSDAS Registration and Information Book*.

MCAT Student Manual, Association of American Medical Colleges, Washington, DC, 1991, $20.00.

The Official Guide for GMAT Review, Graduate Management Admission Council, McLean, VA, $15.95.

TEACHING (CHAPTER 11)

Chalking It Up, Advice to a New TA, by Bruce Reznick, McGraw-Hill, 1988, out of print.

REFERENCE ADDRESSES

ADDRESSES, POSTAL, E-MAIL AND INTERNET

Allied Health Professions Admission Test. Administered by The Psychological Corporation, see address on page 244.

American Association of Dental Schools Application Service (AADSAS). For applications, tel: 800 253-2237,
e-mail: aadsas.appl @jhu.edu/apply.html

American Bar Association—Section on Legal Education and Admissions to the Bar. Internet: http://www.abanet.org/legaled

American Dental Association, Department of Testing Services, 211 E. Chicago Ave., Suite 1840, Chicago, IL 60611-2678, tel: 312 440-2689.

American Medical College Application Service (AMCAS), 2450 N Street NW, Suite 201, Washington, DC 20037-1131, tel: 202 828-0600, Internet: http://www.aamc.org/stuapps/start.html

American Psychological Association, 1200 17th St. NW, Washington, DC 20036, tel: 202 336-5500. Internet site for graduate student information: http://www.apa.org/students/gradmenu.html

Association of American Medical Colleges, 11 Dupont Circle, NW, Washington, DC 20036. Internet: http://www.aamc.org This page has information about loans for medical students, and electronic application software.

Council of Graduate Schools, tel: 202 223-3791. Internet: http://www.cgsnet.org and http://www.cgsnet.org/student.html The latter site has useful information and good links.

Educational Testing Service, P.O. Box 6000, Princeton, NJ 08541-6000. General inquiries: 609 771-7670, e-mail: gre-info@ets.org, Internet: http://www.ets.org and http://www.gre.org

FastWEB is a database of funding information and includes information on government support programs.
Internet: http://www.studentservices.com/fastweb/

Federal Student Aid Information Center, P.O. Box 84, Washington, DC 20044.

Financial aid information sponsored by the National Association of Student Financial Aid Administrators. Internet: http://www.finaid.org

Free Application for Federal Student Aid (FAFSA), P.O. Box 84, Washington, DC 20044, tel: 800 433-3243.

GMAT, Educational Testing Service, P.O. Box 6103, Princeton, NJ 08541, tel: 609 771-7330. Internet: http://www.gmat.org

Graduate Management Admissions Council (GMAC), 8300 Greensboro Drive, Suite 750, McLean, VA 22102, tel: 703 749-0131.

Graduate Management Admissions Council (GMAC) Director of M.B.A. Forums, P.O. Box 6101, Princeton, NJ 08541, tel: 800 527-7982.

Graduate Record Examinations, See Educational Testing Service above.

Graduate schools guide, http://number2.com/gre/free/guide/index.html This is a short ranking of graduate schools by subject (Number 2 is a test preparation organization).

Graduate schools listed by subject. A limited list of university departments by subject with addresses, telephone numbers, and some e-mail links is on the Internet at http://www.gradschools.com/search.html

GRE-CAT Registration Center, tel: 800 GRE-CALL

History Departments Around the World. A list of web sites maintained by the American Historical Association: http://chnm.grad.edu/chnm/history/depts/

Kaplan organization. tel: 800 KAP-TEST, e-mail: info@kaplan.com

Law School Admission Council (Law Services), Box 2400, 661 Penn St., Newtown, PA 18940-0977, tel: 215 968-1001, Internet: http://www.lsac.org

Law school information page: http://www.lawschool.com

Law School Resources page on law school financial aid.
Internet: http://www.finaid.org/finaid/focus/law.html

Mark's Picks: http://www.finaid.org/finaid/picks.html. Mark Kantrowitz maintains this financial information page, as well as the Internet page at http://www.finaid.org

Mathematics departments. The Penn State mathematics department maintains a very good list of mathematics departments' sites: http://www.math.psu.edu/MathLists/DeptUSA.html

MBA Loans program sponsored by the Graduate Management Admissions Council, tel: 800 366-6227, e-mail: csn@northstar.org,
Internet: http://www.gmat.org

MCAT Program Office, P.O. Box 4056, Iowa City, IA 52243-4056, tel: 319 337-1357.

Medical students financial aid Internet page (including book lists and loan info): http://www.finaid.org/finaid/focus/medical.html

Miller Analogies Test. Administered by The Psychological Corporation; see address below.

Minorities: National Consortium for Graduate Degrees for Minorities in Engineering and Science, Inc. This site, maintained by the University of Notre Dame, has much useful information. Internet: http://www.nd.edu/~gem/

Minority On-Line Information Service (MOLIS):
Internet: http://www.finaid.org/finaid/focus/minority.html

Optometry Admission Testing Program, 211 E. Chicago Ave., Suite 211, Chicago, IL 60611-2678, tel: 312 440-2693.

Peterson's Graduate and Professional Study/Faculty. The Internet site http://www.petersons.com/graduate has useful information, including lists of departments in most disciplines. Peterson's main site on the Internet is http://www. petersons.com

Pharmacy College Admission Test. Administered by The Psychological Corporation; see address below.

Princeton Review: Internet: http://www.review.com, e-mail: info.tpr@review.com, tel: 800 273-8439.

Princeton Review page on financing law school:
http://www.review.com/faid/law_faid.html.org/finaid/focus/law.html

The Psychological Corporation, 555 Academic Court, San Antonio, TX 78204, tel: 800 622-3231.

Research and Education Association, 61 Ethel Road West, Piscataway, NJ 08854.

Veterinary College Admission Test. Administered by The Psychological Corporation, see address above.

REGIONAL ACCREDITING AGENCIES

Middle States Association of Colleges and Schools
3624 Market Street
Philadelphia, PA 19104
Tel: 215 662-5606
Covers Delaware, District of Columbia, Maryland, New Jersey, New York, Pennsylvania, Puerto Rico, Virgin Islands.

New England Association of Colleges and Schools
209 Burlington Road
Bedford, MA 01730
Tel: 617 271-0022
Covers Connecticut, Maine, Massachusetts, New Hampshire, Rhode Island, Vermont.

North Central Association of Colleges and Schools
30 N. LaSalle St., Suite 2400
Chicago, IL 60602
Tel: 312 263-0456
Covers Arizona, Arkansas, Colorado, Illinois, Indiana, Iowa, Kansas, Michigan, Minnesota, Missouri, Nebraska, New Mexico, North Dakota, Ohio, Oklahoma, South Dakota, West Virginia, Wisconsin, Wyoming.

Northwest Association of Colleges and Schools
3700-B University Way
Seattle, WA 98105
Tel: 206 543-0195
Covers Alaska, Idaho, Montana, Nevada, Oregon, Utah, Washington.

Southern Association of Colleges and Schools
1866 Southern Lane
Decatur, GA 30033
Tel: 404 679-4501
Covers Alabama, Florida, Georgia, Kentucky, Louisiana, Mississippi, North Carolina, South Carolina, Tennessee, Texas, Virginia.

Western Association of Colleges and Schools
Mills College, P.O. Box 9990
Oakland, CA 94613
Tel: 510 632-5000
Covers American Samoa, California, Guam, Hawaii.

SPECIALIZED ACCREDITING AGENCIES

There are thirty-five separate specialized accrediting agencies. They cover the fields of Acupuncture, Allied Health, Architecture, Art and Design, Business, Chiropractic, Dance, Dentistry, Education, Engineering, Environment, Health Services Administration, Interior Design, Journalism and Mass Communication, Law, Marriage and Family Therapy, Medicine, Music, Naturopathic Medicine, Nurse Anesthesia, Nurse Midwifery, Nursing, Occupational Therapy, Optometry, Osteopathic Medicine, Pharmacy, Physical Therapy, Podiatric Medicine, Psychology, Public Health, Rabbinical and Talmudic Education, Speech-Language Pathology and Audiology, Theater, Theology, and Veterinary Medicine. The address of each of these agencies is given in *Peterson's Guide to Professional and Graduate Programs*, Vol 1.

Resolution on Acceptance of Financial Support

The Council of Graduate Schools issued this resolution, which describes the obligations, principally regarding the April 15 deadline, of students who receive an offer of financial aid and of institutions that support the resolution.

RESOLUTION REGARDING GRADUATE SCHOLARS, FELLOWS, TRAINEES AND ASSISTANTS

Acceptance of an offer of financial support (such as a graduate scholarship, fellowship, traineeship, or assistantship) for the next academic year by a prospective or enrolled graduate student completes an agreement that both student and graduate school expect to honor. In that context, the conditions affecting such offers and their acceptance must be defined carefully and understood by all parties.

Students are under no obligation to respond to offers of financial support prior to April 15; earlier deadlines for acceptance of such offers violate the intent of this Resolution. In those instances in which a student accepts an offer before April 15, and subsequently desires to withdraw that acceptance, the student may submit in writing a resignation of the appointment at any time through April 15. However, an acceptance given or left in force after April 15 commits the student not to accept another offer without first obtaining a written release from the institution to which a commitment has been made. Similarly, an offer by an institution after April 15 is conditional on presentation by the student of the written release from any previously accepted offer. It is further agreed by the institutions and organization subscribing to the above Resolution that a copy of this Resolution should accompany every scholarship, fellowship, traineeship, and assistantship offer.

The following list includes CGS members and those institutions which indicated their support of the above Resolution as of January 1993.

Abilene Christian University
Adelphi University
Alabama A&M University
Alfred University
American University
Andrews University
Angelo State University
Appalachian University
Arizona State University
Arkansas State University
Auburn University
Austin Peay State University
Ball State University
Baylor College of Medicine

Baylor University
Boston College
Boston University
Bowling Green State University
Bradley University
Brandeis University
Bridgewater State College
Brigham Young University
Brown University
Bryn Mawr College
California Institute of Technology
California State College, Stanislaus
California State Polytechnic University, Pomona
California State University, Bakersfield
California State University, Fresno
California State University, Fullerton
California State University, Hayward
California State University, Long Beach
California State University, Los Angeles
California State University, Northridge
California State University, Sacramento
California University of Pennsylvania
Case Western Reserve University
Catholic University of America
Central Michigan University
Central Missouri State University
Central State University
Central Washington University
Chicago State University
City College of the City University of New York
City University of New York
Claremont Graduate School
Clark Atlanta University
Clark University
Clemson University
Cleveland State University
College of Saint Rose
College of William & Mary
Colorado School of Mines
Columbia University
Coppin State College
Cornell University
Creighton University
Dartmouth College
DePaul University
Drake University
Drew University
Drexel University
Duke University
Duquesne University

East Carolina University
East Central Oklahoma State
East Tennessee State University
East Texas State University
Eastern Illinois University
Eastern Kentucky University
Eastern Michigan University
Eastern Washington University
Emerson College
Emory University
Emporia State University
Fairleigh Dickinson University
Fielding Institute
Fisk University
Fitchburg State College
Florida Atlantic University
Florida International University
Florida State University
Fordham University
Fort Hays State University
Gallaudet University
Gannon University
George Mason University
George Washington University
Georgetown University
Georgia Institute of Technology
Georgia Southern College
Glassboro State College
Governors State University
Hampton University
Hardin-Simmons University
Harvard University
Hebrew Union College-Jewish Institute of Religion
Hofstra University
Howard University
Idaho State University
Illinois Institute of Technology
Illinois State University
Indiana State University
Indiana University
Indiana University of Pennsylvania
Iona College
Iowa State University
Jackson State University
James Madison University
John Carroll University
John Jay College of Criminal Justice
Johns Hopkins University
Kansas State University
Kent State University
Lamar University

Lehigh University
Loma Linda University
Louisiana State University and A&M College
Louisiana State University Medical Center
Loyola Marymount University
Loyola University of Chicago
Mankato State University
Marquette University
Marshall University
Massachusetts Institute of Technology
McNeese State University
Medical College of Georgia
Medical College of Pennsylvania
Medical College of Wisconsin
Medical University of South Carolina
Memphis State University
Miami University
Michigan State University
Michigan Technological University
Middle Tennessee State University
Midwestern State University
Mississippi College
Mississippi State University
Montana State University
Montclair State College
Morehead State University
Murray State University
National University
Naval Postgraduate School
New Jersey Institute of Technology
New Mexico Institute of Mining and Technology
New Mexico State University
New School of Social Research
New York Medical College
New York University
Niagara University
North Carolina Agricultural and Technical State University
North Carolina State University at Raleigh
North Dakota State University
North Texas State University
Northeast Missouri State University
Northeastern Illinois University
Northeastern University
Northern Arizona University
Northern Illinois University
Northern Michigan University
Northwestern State University of Louisiana

Northwestern University
Nova University
Oakland University
Ohio State University
Ohio University
Oklahoma State University
Old Dominion University
Oregon State University
Pennsylvania State University
Pepperdine University
Pittsburgh State University
Polytechnic University
Princeton University
Purdue University
Queens College of the City University of New York
Rensselaer Polytechnic Institute
Rhode Island College
Rice University
Rockefeller University
Roosevelt University
Russell Sage College
Rutgers, The State University of New Jersey
Sacred Heart University
St. Bonaventure University
St. John's University
Saint Louis University
St. Mary's University
Sam Houston State University
San Diego State University
San Francisco State University
San Jose State University
Sangamon State University
Santa Clara University
Seattle University
Shippensburg University
Sonoma State University
South Carolina State University
South Dakota School of Mines and Technology
South Dakota State University
Southeastern Louisiana University
Southern Illinois University, Carbondale
Southern Illinois University, Edwardsville
Southern Methodist University
Southern University
Southwest Missouri State University
Southwest Texas State University
Stanford University
State University of New York, Albany

State University of New York,
  Binghamton
State University of New York, Buffalo
State University of New York, Stony
  Brook
State University of New York—
  Downstate Medical Center
State University of New York—Upstate
  Medical Center
Stephen F. Austin State University
Stetson University
Stevens Institute of Technology
Syracuse University
Temple University
Tennessee State University
Tennessee Technological University
Texas A&M University
Texas Christian University
Texas Southern University
Texas Tech University
Texas Woman's University
Towson State University
Trenton State University
Trinity University
Tufts University
Tulane University
United States International University
University of Akron
University of Alabama
University of Alabama at Birmingham
University of Alabama in Huntsville
University of Alaska
University of Arizona
University of Arkansas
University of Baltimore
University of Bridgeport
University of California at Berkeley
University of California-Davis
University of California, Irvine
University of California, Los Angeles
University of California, Riverside
University of California, San Diego
University of California, San Francisco
University of California, Santa Barbara
University of California Santa Cruz
University of Central Florida
University of Chicago
University of Cincinnati
University of Colorado at Boulder
University of Colorado at Denver
University of Connecticut
University of Dayton

University of Delaware
University of Denver
University of Detroit
University of the District of Columbia
University of Evansville
University of Florida
University of Georgia
University of Hartford
University of Hawaii
University of Health Sciences/The
  Chicago Medical School
University of Houston
University of Idaho
University of Illinois at Chicago
University of Illinois at Urbana-
  Champaign
University of Iowa
University of Kansas
University of Louisville
University of Lowell
University of Maine
University of Maryland
University of Massachusetts at Amherst
University of Massachusetts-Boston
University of Miami
University of Michigan
University of Minnesota
University of Mississippi
University of Missouri, Columbia
University of Missouri, Rolla
University of Missouri, St. Louis
University of Montana
University of Nebraska, Lincoln
University of Nevada, Las Vegas
University of Nevada, Reno
University of New Hampshire
University of New Haven
University of New Mexico
University of New Orleans
University of North Carolina, Chapel Hill
University of North Carolina, Charlotte
University of North Carolina, Greensboro
University of North Carolina, Wilmington
University of North Dakota
University of North Texas
University of Northern Colorado
University of Northern Iowa
University of Notre Dame
University of Oklahoma
University of Oregon
University of the Pacific
University of Pennsylvania

University of Pittsburgh
University of Rhode Island
University of Rochester
University of San Francisco
University of Santa Clara
University of Scranton
University of South Carolina
University of South Dakota
University of South Florida
University of Southern California
University of Southern Maine
University of Southern Mississippi
University of Southwestern Louisiana
University of Tennessee, Chattanooga
University of Tennessee, Knoxville
University of Tennessee, Martin
University of Tennessee, Memphis
  Center for the Health Sciences
University of Texas at Arlington
University of Texas at Austin
University of Texas at Dallas
University of Texas at San Antonio
University of Texas Health Science
  Center at Houston Graduate School of
  Biomedical Sciences
University of Texas Health Science
  Center at San Antonio Graduate
  School of Biomedical Sciences
University of Texas Medical Branch at
  Galveston Graduate School of
  Biomedical Sciences
University of Toledo
University of Tulsa
University of Utah
University of Vermont
University of Virginia

University of Washington
University of Wisconsin-Eau Claire
University of Wisconsin-Green Bay
University of Wisconsin-Madison
University of Wisconsin-Milwaukee
University of Wisconsin-Oshkosh
University of Wisconsin-Stout
University of Wyoming
Utah State University
Vanderbilt University
Villanova University
Virginia Commonwealth University
Virginia Polytechnic Institute & State
  University
Wake Forest University
Washington State University
Washington University
Wayne State College
Wayne State University
Wesleyan University
West Chester University
West Texas State University
West Virginia University
Western Carolina University
Western Illinois University
Western Kentucky University
Western Michigan University
Western Washington University
Westfield State College
Wichita State University
Worcester Polytechnic Institute
Worcester State College
Wright State University
Xavier University
Yale University
Youngstown State University

Council of Graduate Schools
One Dupont Circle, N.W., Suite 430
Washington, DC 20036-1173
Reprinted by permission.

INDEX